'Bruce's love of Country is resoundi[n]
that this book and his work with the Black Duck team has been
profoundly cleansing for a man who has faced numerous challenges
in his life after *Dark Emu*. His connection to place, land and Country
is at the core of his remarkable resilience. Bruce gets right into the
belly of the land and storytelling, a medicine this country needs.'

—Stephen Page

'Bruce invites us onto the land that changed the man behind the book
that changed the nation.'

—Narelda Jacobs

'This brilliant book gives a real insight into the minds and lives of
Bruce and Lyn and the impact *Dark Emu* had on both of them.'

—Tony Armstrong

'Bruce and Lyn so eloquently bring us into intimate contact with the
land and our beautiful culture – reminding us all of the rich history
that Australia holds.'

—Allira Potter

This book is dedicated to
Grandmother and Grandfather,
Mother and Father.

A Year at Yumburra

BLACK DUCK

BRUCE PASCOE

WITH LYN HARWOOD

T&H

First published in Australia in 2024
by Thames & Hudson Australia Pty Ltd
11 Central Boulevard, Portside Business Park
Port Melbourne, Victoria 3207
ABN: 72 004 751 964

thamesandhudson.com.au

27 26 25 24   5 4 3 2 1

Thames & Hudson Australia wishes to acknowledge that Aboriginal and Torres Strait Islander
people are the first storytellers of this nation and the Traditional Custodians of the land on
which we live and work. We acknowledge their continuing culture and pay respect to Elders past
and present.

ISBN 978-1-760-76311-4 (paperback)
ISBN 978-1-760-76320-6 (ebook)

A catalogue record for this
book is available from the
National Library of Australia

Cover design: Andy Warren
Cover artwork: Lyn Harwood
Typesetting: Cannon Typesetting
Editing: Melissa-Jane Fogarty
Project manager: Shannon Grey

Printed and bound in Australia by McPherson's Printing Group

Contents

CONTENTS

Map illustration by Chris Solazzini

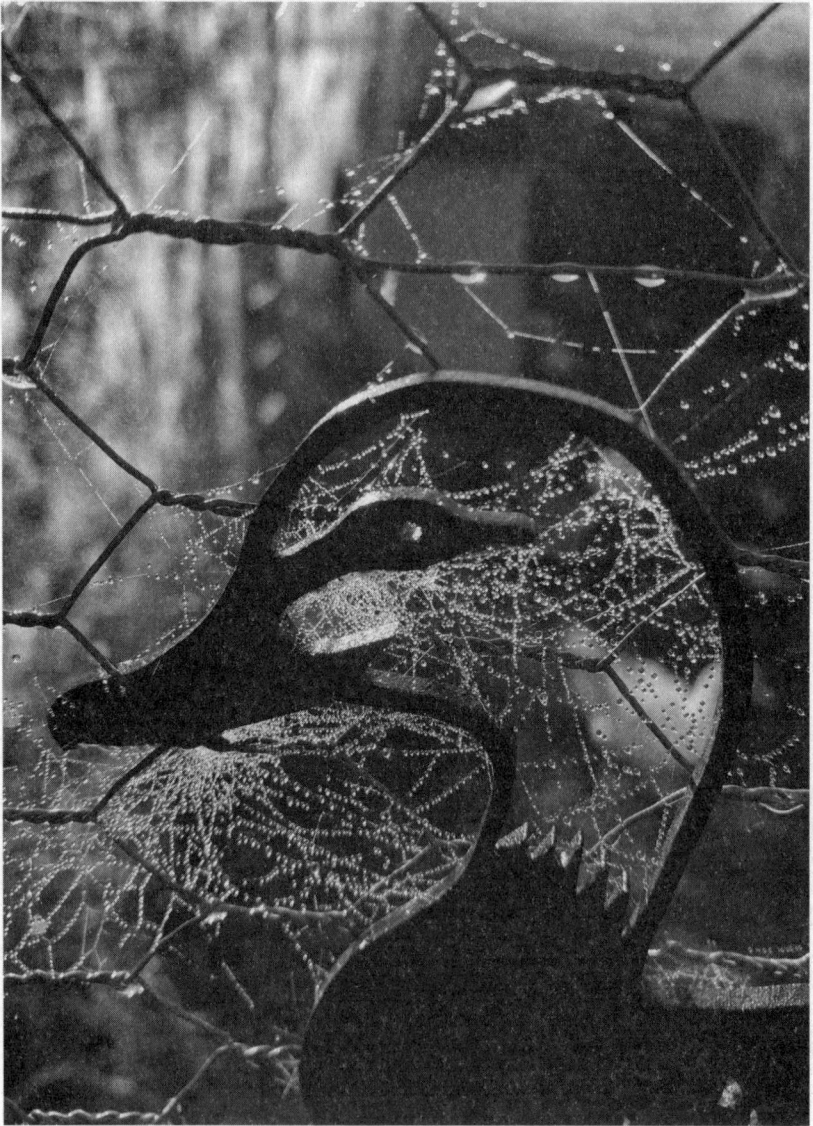

Yumburra, Black Duck

The Black Duck

At Yumburra, on Yuin Country close to Mallacoota, Aboriginal peoples cultivate the traditional Aboriginal grasses and tubers. Black Duck grows over forty Aboriginal foods with the goal of redeveloping traditional food growing and country management processes for the economic benefit of Aboriginal peoples and Country.

'We want to tell the story of our lands. For a long time, the story of traditional agriculture was buried. Stories from elders across the country were ignored. We respect the keepers of these stories and acknowledge their resilience. Our stories come from a time when stories began, and we are now transforming these stories into new opportunities for Aboriginal people as part of the journey towards food sovereignty.'

—Black Duck Foods

An Introduction to Our Country

An Owlet-nightjar is more butterfly than bird, more spirit than being, less weight than a handful of grapes. Pale fairy of the night.

I hear their soft churring almost every night but can count the times I have seen one on the fingers of two hands. It is like seeing a large moth fluttering silently in the dark. Our people say they hold the woman spirit. Their eyes are huge, doe-like, but that description belies their huge responsibility.

I turned the corner onto the Gipsy Point Road on a September day at three in the morning and there she was on the road in front of me, those huge eyes questioning my appearance at that hour, the hour of true dreams or restless wakefulness. I stopped and considered my response.

You're back, she said. And that's how it felt. I opened the door a fraction so that she could hear the click and it was enough for her to flutter into the Melaleucas beside the road.

I shut the door and drove on carefully to make sure I could avoid a collision with any startled roo or wallaby. At the end of the road the little town nestled against the dark water where three great salt rivers meet. Wallagaraugh, Jinoor and Maramingo. Is it a town if it's without a shop of any kind? The sleeping houses were unconcerned by semantics.

On the bank of the river there were thirty or more kangaroos. I nodded, yes, that's about how I remembered it. I thought the property would be on my right and so I parked the car and stepped out to prove the theory.

I was anxious to see if the old jetty was still there and yes, there it was. A Night Heron was dozing on the handrail. The land was sold in that instant.

The moon over the jetty at Gipsy Point

Grief

When our son seemed destined for university in the city I could see Lyn get twitchy, rattled, cups jittered precariously in her hands, her eyes were distracted. It was grief.

She is a natural architect, forever conscious of light and warmth and comforting spaces. I suggested we begin the search for land on which to build a holiday house. Her holiday house. We only had enough for a cheap block. Remoteness made blocks cheap.

We tried Tasmania but the cost of travel to and from the island was prohibitive. We were speechless at the cost of properties on the Glenelg River, dismayed by the winds of South Australia, the ugly clutter that the Queensland coast had become. Then Lyn found a block for sale at Gipsy Point. I looked closely at the dim photograph and figured I knew exactly where the block was located. On the Jinoor River, site of the best pub in Australia, although the photo managed to avoid inclusion of either the pub or the river. The selling point seemed to be the stump of a fallen wattle.

I picked up the car keys and swag and stuffed two t-shirts and a pair of undies in a plastic bag and headed east. It was a ten-hour drive from where we lived in the Otways, so I had to swag it in a bush rest stop near Stratford. I woke at midnight and stirred up the old Subaru and drove on. I had lived in the district of Gipsy Point in the seventies and early eighties. After my uncle showed the place to me in 1963, I promised myself I would return there one day. On Country.

I made it back in 1973 but with a daughter and unhappy wife. In Paradise. I had never seen a place so beautiful, never felt so at home, so viscerally attached to the land. The marriage didn't last, couldn't have, and I lost the land. Dragged myself to Melbourne but knew I couldn't survive inside paling fences.

I met Lyn, or rather heard her laughter in a stairwell, and realised I hadn't laughed in a long while. We exchanged observations of birds and leaves and not much later stood together watching horses in a paddock. She invited me to pull up a concrete slab in her backyard and I accepted because it was the best offer I'd had in years.

We visited the Otway Coast and I watched in amazement as she crawled through the tea tree bowers searching for orchids. This is different, I thought. Someone connected to Country. We bought a block at Cape Otway and lived in a tiny second-hand van while we built a house on an old sand dune in a manna gum forest.

Jack was soon on the way. But in the blink of an eye seventeen years had passed and Lyn was fumbling cups and tea towels and not quite closing doors. I know, I thought, I'll keep her busy.

Gipsy Point isn't busy but it's warm. One day I was drilling screws into galvanised beams to fix decking timbers, sweat was dripping onto my father's old Black & Decker drill. I knocked off and went down to the jetty, stripped off my sodden shirt and dived into the river. Halfway through the dive I thought, Hang on, it's August.

Gipsy is warm, Cape Otway is not.

But Cape Otway had a lot of Lomandra and that's what the old ladies wanted, the weavers. Men and women came from all over the western district to collect Lomandra leaves and have a cup of tea, sometimes more tea leaves than weaving leaves. But eventually I'd be dragooned into the harvest of the tough leaves the women would soak and dry, soak and dry to make them pliable enough for basket and eel trap making.

Elders from the district needed help with cultural protection and they couldn't be too fussy about where that help came from.

They'd heard stories about my family. They'd told me stories of theirs but they were alarmed by my ignorance. Despite this their patience was limitless. Aunty Joyce predicted accurately that I would find some family in Tasmania and Aunty Bunta, even more accurately, thought that family would be connected to Victorians. For both women the reverse had been true. Uncle Ivan listened and listened, a thoroughly decent man, but warned me that before looking for family I had to learn the real history of the country, the black history. Uncle Banjo insisted that pale-skinned Aboriginal people had a role in community, after all, no one had ever been found to be half pregnant; you either were or you weren't. No fence-sitting.

They sent me back to the library with tantalising suggestions of the Eumeralla war, the militias based at Pirron Yallock, the fastnesses of the Stony Rises, the many murders and massacres everywhere, including Cape Otway.

The Wathaurong asked me to take over the research for the *Dictionary of Wathawoorroong* because the incumbent researcher had accepted a promotion to National Parks; the fate of so many young and smart Blackfellas; being snatched by government as soon as community had trained them to undertake responsible positions. Aboriginal communities are unofficial and unpaid training institutes.

Aunty Zelda insisted she attend my library visits so she could teach me how to use my antennae. We visited almost every library, museum or history association in the western district. She liked the Geelong Historical Records Centre because they had the best cafe across the road. In those days Birregurra was a complete disappointment in that regard so she was careful to pack a thermos.

She trained me to be a jewel thief and a rat detector. She could sense in the first thirty seconds if the staff were going to be uninformed, uncooperative or downright racist. Sadly, more often the latter two.

She would engage all the staff in some search for the athletic exploits of one of her relations in boxing, running, bicycle races or football. Black people dominated Victorian sport up to about 1930. 'Did you know,' she would say to a staff member caught like a rabbit in the spotlight, 'he won that race against all the Olympic champions on a fixed wheel postie's bike?'

I think the postie's bike was Aunty Zelda's invention for dramatic effect but it was certainly fixed wheel and it was reported in the press. 'And did you know he won that 100-yard dash three times, but they always gave the cup to the first white man to cross the line?' That also was a true story. 'And did you know that the trainers at Fitzroy footy club wouldn't give Doug Nicholls a rub down because they didn't want to touch black skin?' Well, it was my father who told me that last story, but it was the sort of thing that Aunty Zelda would use to get the shamed librarian to find the documents she wanted.

Meanwhile, I was free to access the documents she really wanted me to see. She knew the rest like the back of her hand. But she provided cover for my searches. Once at the Public Record Office my search for documents about the Great Victorian War was being hampered by a factotum who thought he was still on the frontier.

'Oh look,' Aunt chortled from a corner of the Record Office, 'here they are, they were here all the time and you must have forgotten.' She was a bit of a witch in many ways. She pinned those people down until the armpits of their office shirts darkened with suppressed rage.

Once at the Colac Information Centre I was asking about the fort that had been built out beyond Irrewillipe. 'Oh, no fort ever built here,' the ruddy-cheeked RSL badge was saying, 'no, no fort here.' Aunt spun around and faced him. 'You know the one, the one with the loopholes for windows.' I stared at her in amazement. How did she know about loopholes? But when I turned back to old silver-short-back-and-sides, a loyalist's haircut, I had no doubt he knew what they were and knew exactly what building she was referring to.

I visited that building several times to measure the gun embrasures, the perfect shape within which to swivel a gun. Then I went back to the Information Centre to show the photos to old short-back-and-sides. He tried to bluster about Cobb & Co. horse stables but a horse doesn't need to swivel to breathe air. We both knew what a gun embrasure was and against whom the guns were pointed.

I wrote a story about those windows in my short story collection, *Salt*. Travels with Aunty Zelda and company also influenced my books *Cape Otway*, *Convincing Ground* and *Dark Emu*.

The latter two were written in a little office Lyn and I and some mates built beside the Gipsy house that Lyn designed with Johnny Grunden, the best damn double bass player in southern Australia.

Convincing Ground gained a fervent readership, keen to learn what Aunty Zelda and Uncle Ivan knew, but it was *Dark Emu* that was adopted by Australia like a new anthem. It was obvious a year out from publication that it would sell better than any other of the twenty-five books I had written to that point. At one lecture at the Australian National University the room was full of professors and, while some of the elbow patch brigade wanted to accuse me of sedition, others scribbled down other references I needed to read. Insurrection had been abroad for some time.

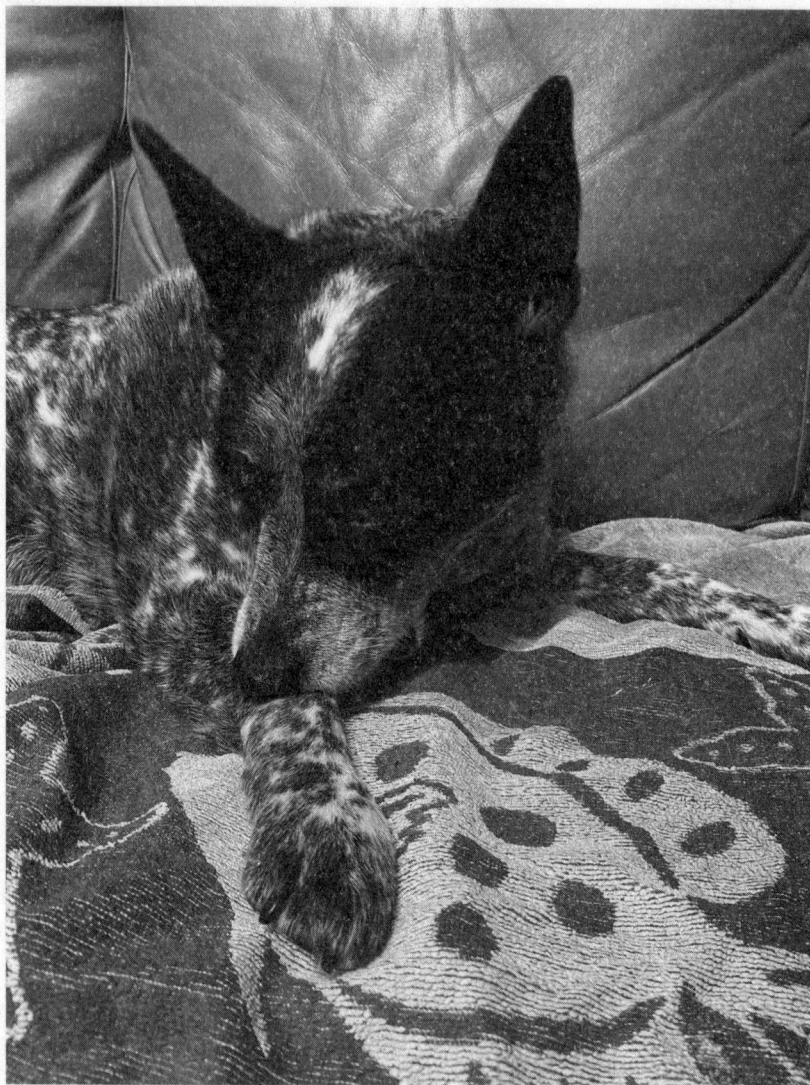

Wangarabell (Bell), Spirit dog

The book had me travelling from state to state, county to country, town hall to town hall, but it tested Lyn and me to the limit. It came to a point where she could barely sit in the room when some stranger came to discuss the bloody emu.

We separated in 2017, three years after *Dark Emu* was published, and live in separate houses to this day. The last of our two shared dogs is dying on the couch as I write these words. The famous Wangarabell, spirit dog of the Bidwell-Maap.

The fracture between Lyn and I was deep, and the momentum of *Dark Emu* increased the distance despite the fact that we remained best friends and supporters.

In 2021 we went on a holiday together and did all the things we'd always done; beach walks, bird watching, reading and talking around the stove. A few weeks earlier I saw Lyn fall and my reaction was very telling. I thought she had done herself some real damage. It wrenched my guts and it told me a lot about the depth of our connection. We reaffirmed our bonds a few months later on a lonely beach at Wilsons Promontory.

Lyn hadn't wanted to have anything to do with the farm at Yumburra, mainly because of the enormous physical and financial drain it would have on us, but I felt I had to buy the farm to show that Yuin people were still connected to our old foods. The Yorta Yorta decision by Justice Olney in 2002 that the people's culture and rights had been washed away by the tide of history shocked me to the core. Once bakers and restaurateurs had joined the *Emu*'s bandwagon, I could see a second dispossession racing toward us.

And without a home, I bought the farm. I tried to buy superior land on the highway near Eden, but it was too expensive, so I ended up with Yumburra, a remote farm in a remote district of Far East Gippsland. My workload was ridiculous and Lyn, despite her doubts, helped with the administration and later joined the Black Duck board.

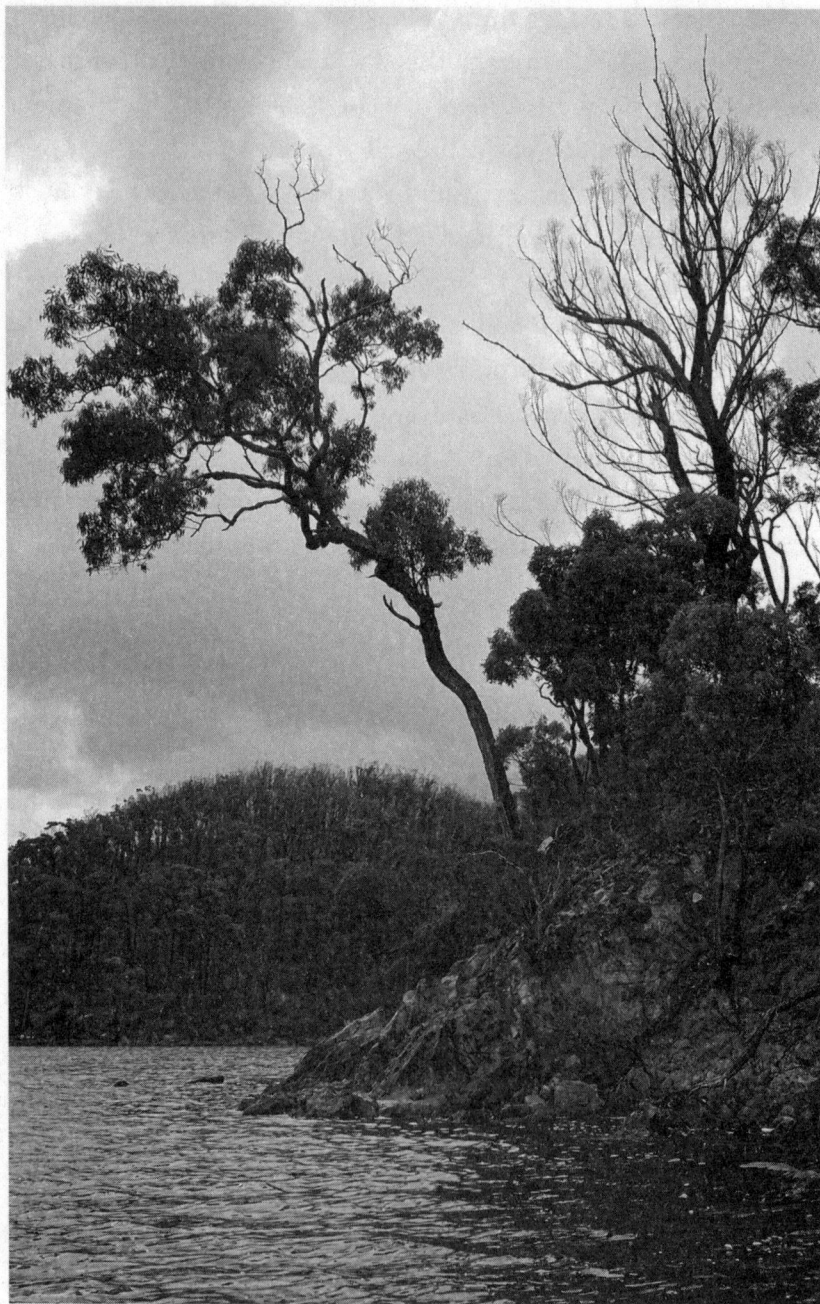

The Wallagaraugh River

Her hard work and persistence was a big factor in us being able to insist on running the company as an Aboriginal business instead of a token effort run by self-serving white entrepreneurs.

My connection to the land goes back a long way. Around 1963 my Uncle Alf had introduced me to the Wallagaraugh River.

He was a ratbag, drinker, swearer, smoker, gambler, blasphemer, driver of a grey Pontiac, everything my father wasn't. I loved my father, but was entranced by the bravado and stories of my uncle's wild life. And his close association with my grandfather; a drinker, swearer, country sideshow huckster, driver of a horse and cart.

Uncle introduced me to people he said were our family as we rode in Hancock's fish truck. This life was a revelation, the antithesis of respectability, the thing the rest of the family so badly wanted.

My father also took me to Mallacoota (Coota) but in a Morris Oxford rather than a fish truck. The Oxford could not compete with the glamour of a fish truck.

It was a long road to get back to the Wallagaraugh after those first visits, but this is the story of a year in her company, the company of Yumburra, the Black Duck, supreme spiritual being of Yuin Country.

Late Summer

Fly away seeds of Murnong

The mornings smell of dry grass and the Yellow-faced Honeyeater's
chickup–chickup call rings through the forest.

Gipsy Point

Gipsy Point is spelt with an 'i' because the skipper of the boat of that name couldn't spell. She collected stores of wattle bark from the district and took them to Melbourne for sale to the tanneries. When I bought the farm, Green Range, on the banks of the Maramingo Creek in 1975, there were still bales of wattle bark tied with sisal rope waiting for a collection that never came after chemical leather tanning took over from wattle bark.

The bales had been made by Old Freeman who lived along Freemans Track. Some say he was an Aboriginal Yuin man. His neighbour, Caleb Cook, from Green Range, also collected bark and eventually sold his land to James Hardie and company, who were wattle bark traders and tanners before they began their asbestos adventure.

The last wattle bark jetty in the Backwater, upstream from Gipsy Point, was pulled down around 2015, a sad day for the white history of the town. When I first came to the district, I found wattle and Melaleuca poles stacked neatly in the shallows. The logs encouraged cobberers (Teredo worms) to burrow inside them. It was a favourite food of local Aboriginal people and tastes like oyster.

Who put those stacks there? Jinoor Jack, Uncle Muns? These two prominent Aboriginal men spent a lot of time around these rivers. We might never know who created the stacks but it was a comfort to see them there. There's a lot of history that goes unnoticed around here.

The Gipsy Point Hotel was pulled down around 1998 and replaced with tourist accommodation. The district lost its favourite pub and social identity. Lyn and I bought the land in 2001, and when the house was finished in 2004, we would go down to the public jetty every Friday night to eat a meal and have a drink. Soon it became a town ritual.

In winter we have seven to eight stoics, in summer when our families are with us, there might be fifty. The town only has around fifteen residents; if they are all home.

These days it is shocking to think how many we have lost of that company over the two decades of the jetty pub. The park bench we got Robert Stevens to build for us is now covered in plaques for the old, missing friends. Bob is a local furniture maker and we'll need to engage his services again quite soon!

When we gathered on 1 January 2022, we were aware of the departed but exhilarated by the clutter of children storming in to the tables to devour the chips and chicken but avoiding the salads as if they were radioactive.

Three of our grandkids were there and, even though they knew few of the gang of town grandchildren, they were soon bombing off the jetty and using my boat, *Nadgee IV*, as the staging point for further sorties. They had plastic rafts and boogie boards 30 metres from the jetty so that there was a never-ending stream of swimmers, divers, climbers and fetchers.

I was mesmerised by the beauty of the scene, filled with warmth by the good humour and communal care they shared for each other. It was an unforgettable night because I not only saw growth in my grandchildren, but I also witnessed the decency and maturity of all the other Summer Gipsy Kids. I'll never forget the humanity of it. Wild children watched over by the ones who loved them and they, in turn, watching over those smaller or meeker than themselves.

The babies, too small to risk in the water, were goggle-eyed with wonder at the antics of the older children and struggled to be free. Wiser arms held them and offered them wonderful things to eat and, when that failed, a song or a toy, but those babies' eyes swivelled back to the jetty at every shriek and explosion of water. They were crazed with aquatic ambition.

Bunjil

I took *Nadgee* back to the farm, and when I got back to the house Bunjil was sitting on the edge of the duck yard but fortunately had not been able to get in. I have to be respectful and polite to Bunjil, the Wedge-tailed Eagle, but she had been testing me. The previous week she had taken two ducks and four ducklings.

Ruski, one of the ducks, had a deep wound to the chest which we fixed with Pippin's antibiotic spray. Pippin is a horse, not a chemist. I couldn't believe Ruski had survived. The eagle had grabbed her in her talons, which went straight through her wing and into her chest. The ducks went off the lay immediately and were glassy-eyed with horror for weeks.

Over the year the eagles had killed five ducks and six ducklings despite the various coverings I had erected for their yard. I erected a chicken wire roof over the entire area but not before Mick, the mad road builder from Cann River, discovered an eagle in the yard and captured it in his coat. He took a video of himself unveiling the

Bunjil, the Wedge-tailed Eagle

giant bird on the back of his ute as if he was a famous prestidigitator. The bird was huffy with disdain and wheeled away in great chagrin.

As usual, the duck yard was a charnel house. I had bought the ducks to entertain the grandkids when they stayed with me during the Covid lockdowns but when they left, they left the ducks too. All the ducks had names so there were some strained conversations after every Bunjil visit.

Earlier in the year I returned to the farm from working interstate and found three eagles in the duck yard and a trail of death. The birds stood up to the height of my shoulder and were a daunting pack. That year's young was with its parents but the look they gave me was full of defiance.

I had to tear down all the bird netting I had installed, yes, alright, of course it would never have done the job, but bird netting is cheap and quick and I'm time poor. I had to herd the eagles toward the clear space above them. The first leapt to the top rail, more than 3 metres, in a single bound. It felt like having a vulture above me. The other two were harder to encourage but soon I was able to turn my attention to installing more substantial wire and soothing the ducks.

The ducks are constantly alert

It helped to take the carcass of the drake from the roof above them.

I took all the dead birds and spread them on the ground. The eagles watched on with contempt and fury but next morning all the dead were gone. The eagles still check out the strength of the yard roof every summer when the entreaties of that year's young get too persistent. The high-pitched eer eer eer is a constant sound in the warm months.

Grasses

I checked the grasses on the south hill paddock and then we all went to harvest Murnong seed. For $5 a bag, the grannies are very enthusiastic. But there is a mountain of seed to collect from the daisies and lilies. The seed will soon go into tubes ready for planting into the gardens in April and May.

In summer we also harvest Buru Ngalluk (Kangaroo Grass), Garrara Ngalluk (Spear Grass) and Mamadyan Ngalluk (Dancing Grass), thresh it and mill it into flour. It makes beautiful bread.

The Old People's tubers, Murnong (Yam Daisy) and Munyang (Vanilla Lily), have delicious roots, so we are trying to ensure these superb grains and tubers are grown and harvested by Aboriginal people. It is important that we demonstrate that we have maintained contact with our food culture. We employ mostly Yuin people from Eden and Bega. Terry, Nathan and Chris are long-term employees and all deeply involved in culture.

Terry Hayes has been here from day one. He worked on the building of the enclosed gardens. Terry is a Yuin man and part of the Gurandgi lore group. His Mumbullah and Hayes family both have important cultural links. Nathan Lygon is also a Yuin man. I knew Nathan through work on Yuin language and our membership with the Twofold Aboriginal Corporation.

Spear grass

Chris Harris is a Nyaampa man and I met Chris when he was working for Mundabaa, the Twofold Aboriginal Corporation building group, who built the new rooms on the farm house. Chris was plastering but kept on asking what we were doing on the farm. When I asked if he was interested in working for us he jumped at the chance. He drives an hour and a half every day to get to work. That's dedication.

Chris and Terry milling flour

Black Duck Foods was established as a basis for this social enter-
prise. It was purchased and established with the funds raised from
selling an old house and the income from book sales of *Dark Emu*. The
aim is to grow and sell food, but the underlying ambition is to protect
Aboriginal food sovereignty and create real employment opportunities.

Summer is incredibly busy for Black Duck because so much of
the food needs to be harvested in that season, but amongst all the
harvesting there is another dominant pattern to family life. It is called
swimming. I bribe the kids to help me harvest seed while the farm
crew are on leave, but after the seed harvesting we all go down to
the river and the old stand-up paddle board is again the venue for
gymnastics and piracy.

Yumburra

The farm is on the Wallagaraugh river and 2 kilometres downstream
it merges with the Jinoor into which the Maramingo has already
flowed. The three salt rivers to which my book *Salt* is dedicated are
also the subject of a song the Yuin Gurandgi sing to celebrate this side
of the Great Dividing Range.

Yuin Gurandgi are the cultural lore group established by Uncle
Max Harrison. There are over 150 lore men and a growing group
of women. It is not the only lore group in the south-east but it is
probably the biggest and most active. Uncle Max led an active and
successful life but toward the end of it he worried about how Yuin
lore would continue. He began to collect local men around him so
that he could impart the lessons given to him by Uncle Muns.

The farm is on the southern Yuin Country to which my Uncle
Alf and Dad introduced me when I was a boy. The farm has a prominent bluff above the river, which I noticed way back in 1963 without

realising its importance. The two coolamon scars at the edge of the clearing were obvious enough but the knoll also had an Aboriginal history. When I inspected it more closely, I noticed some stones scattered in a corner of the clearing, and when I showed those stones to Uncle Max he said he'd seen something similar before and he thought he could put it back together.

We had twenty-five Gurandgi staying on the property at the time so we re-established the arrangement and found that it aligns perfectly east and west.

Below the knoll, or buna, a shallow creek joins the Wallagaraugh and in the middle of the river there is a sandbar, often exposed at low tide and patrolled by two plovers, Birran Durran Durran.

Old George Johnson, the first beef farmer and logger to live on the property after the original inhabitants had been evicted, had a jetty that reached into the creek, a very safe anchorage. The jetty survived many floods in the seventies and eighties but when I came back to the rivers it had collapsed.

I brought a chain and my old Case International tractor down to the river, and by making a loop around the furthermost timbers I was able to lift it gently with the hydraulics of the tractor. There were some timbers missing but it had been constructed out of Grey Box poles and planks. Grey Box is incredibly tough timber. Be careful trying to hammer a 6-inch nail into box because the hammer is likely to rebound.

In the seventies I had a farm on the Maramingo (fish spear) Creek and my neighbours, the perpetually supportive Becker family, helped me build a bridge across the Glue Pot Creek to give me access to the old overgrown farm I had bought.

In 2016 I attended a fire on the property as part of the Country Fire Authority (CFA), but when the fire was controlled I took the opportunity to go back to the bridge. I got a large screwdriver from the truck and got beneath the bridge and whacked the screwdriver into the timber. I nearly broke my wrist. Grey Box. Fifty years later but still as sound as when those poles were dropped in place.

With a couple of new poles I was able to stabilise Old George's jetty and with saved timbers from an old jetty at Gipsy Point I was able to re-plank it. It now serves as home for *Nadgee IV* and the water sports of my grandkids.

Boats

I bought the original *Nadgee* from Frank Buckland of Sunny Corner in Mallacoota. Frank had been a lake net fisherman but by the seventies was 'resting', hiring out tourist boats and recovering furniture and livestock when the Jinoor was in flood.

He was a rascal too. He told tourists that his boats ran on salt water. He would demonstrate by pouring saltwater into the tank. The old Simplex motor started without trouble. Tourists thought he was Christ. He offered to walk on water but couldn't because he'd neglected to bring his sandals.

Saltwater is heavier than petrol and sinks to the bottom of the tank. When there is too little fuel to reach the outlet of the fuel line, a little saltwater will bring up the level of the petrol and the motor can use fuel it couldn't access before. But like most Buckland stories, don't try this at home, or alone.

Frank told me he had bought the boat in Narooma, on the south coast of NSW, and sailed it down the coast and brought it over the bar at Mallacoota. When net fishing in the Mallacoota Lakes was being wound back, the *Nadgee* entered retirement in the Narrows, the connecting channel between Mallacoota's two lakes.

Frank recognised someone foolish enough to want to restore an 18-foot wooden boat and sold it to me. He didn't exactly clap his hands but he had the air about him of someone who thought he'd never have to scrape and paint the bottom of an old large boat ever again.

Nadgee lived for many years on the lakes and rivers of Mallacoota but when the motor needed repair, I beached her under the Wallagaraugh River bridge near Lennie Johnson's farm, George's brother. The *Nadgee* disappeared.

'Flood took her,' Lennie told me. We looked at each other dead-pan. There hadn't been enough rain to wash a leaf from the bank but by Len's terms the boat had been there too long; and disappeared. Part of the Johnson broken farm revenue recovery policy perhaps. My fault, never leave a lovely boat alone. I gave the motor to Billy Bruce, but it and he are a different book.

I bought *Nadgee II* from an Aboriginal family in Geelong but she was so old, and the trailer older, that when I towed her to Mallacoota the trailer mudguards rested on the tyres for support and the rubber tried to ignite.

Anyway, that boat came to a sudden stop in Mallacoota's Bottom Lake some years later and Dicky Morris, outboard mechanic nonpareil, had only one word to describe her condition, cactus. I gave the hull to an Aboriginal family in Eden whose forbear had played for Richmond. Sufficient payment.

Nadgee III was a lovely boat but she had a broken transom amongst a few other issues like engine failure and fiberglass necrosis. I took her to Bairnsdale and traded (gave) her in on an old Whittley 5.3 metre half cab. Many of you are sick of boat stats by now but you have to understand that boats are dear to my heart. Anything that floats is precious. *Nadgee IV* is in good health so there will be little need to mention it again.

January is the season of young eagles. Every year the insistent cry of eer eer eer resounds in the valleys. Ducks get nervous, Birran Durran Durran (Masked Lapwing or plover) takes to the air to chastise the young bird.

When Birran Durran Durran calls, everyone – animals and humans – look to the sky. The humans will also check the track for visitors. Birran Durran Durran raises the alarm for everyone about everything. Dogs learn that they need not bark.

In these warm months, mullet mob in schools in the golden shallows and the grasses become blond. Mornings are warm with a minimal dew. You sniff the air for smoke.

Kangaroo Grass hangs in florets

Those long summer days swimming, listening to the cries of the grandkids mingling with those of Golden Whistlers, Yellow-faced Honeyeaters and Crimson Honeyeaters are also harvest days and while the Buru Ngalluk (Kangaroo Grass) seed hangs in the floret we have to harvest the paddocks.

The grass that summer was in top condition and I was struck by the numbers of orchids amongst the crop. There was a beautiful pale Hyacinth Orchid at the edge of the south boundary and it was uplifting just to pass it with every rotation around the crop.

We do knock the heads off a few orchids, but as most reproduce from the bulb it is not the problem many might think. And, in any case, when I bought the place there were no orchids to be seen. Cattle had eaten all the flowers, all the rushes, most of the cumbungi, and I didn't realise there was Water Ribbon on the place until a few weeks after the cattle had been removed. We underestimate the floral price we pay for having such a big hard-hoofed ruminant in this country.

Uncle Max

Uncle Max Harrison is the great-grandson of the single survivor of a massacre of Aboriginal people on the Brodribb River in Far East Gippsland in the 1850s. This incident doesn't appear in the various histories written about these killings because there is no official, police or government, record, but the event is indelibly etched into the memory of local Aboriginal people. Descendants of the perpetrators remember it too.

It took us fifteen years of searching to locate the site. It was known to some white families but never divulged. One old white man, devoted to Uncle Max's pursuit, kept up a relentless round of conversations amongst the holders of that knowledge until he wore

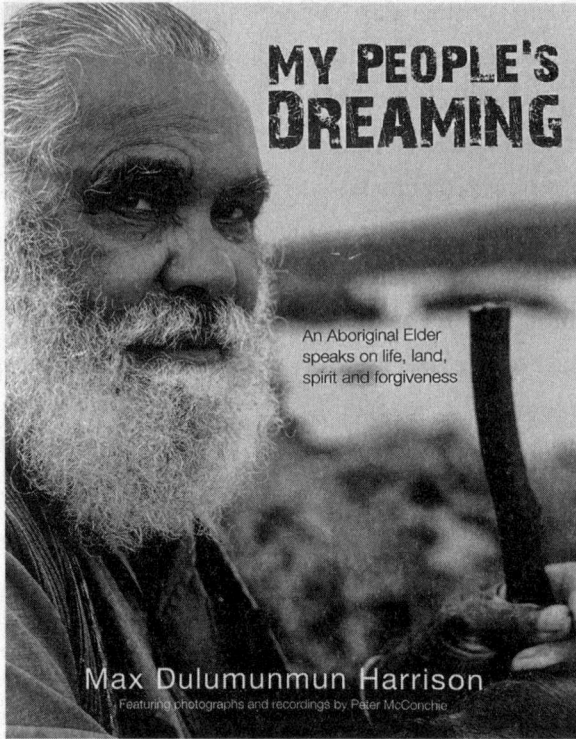

Book cover photo of Uncle Max Harrison (Peter McConchie)

them down, or they simply got sick of seeing him across their kitchen table, his map spread out before them and his lips flap flap flapping.

Eventually one of them pointed to a position on the map and that was that, Lenny Marlo had found the site. All Gurandgi owe a lot to Lenny, the wise old farmer, horticulturalist and lore man.

Thanks to Lenny, Uncle Max was able to visit the place in 2018 and find the exact location of the elimination of all but one of his family. He took us back there for a ceremony in 2019. We cleared the ground and conducted the appropriate ceremony while a Sea Eagle stared down at us from the top of a huge eucalypt for the whole seven hours of the ritual.

That night descendants of the perpetrators came and spoke to the seventy Gurandgi and family assembled at Cape Conran. 'You could have heard a pin drop' is a very overused expression, but on that night that description was perfect for a group that included half a dozen babies and a dozen teenagers.

When Uncle Max invited the families of the perpetrators I doubted that any would turn up, but one family did and it taught me that Uncle's heart and mind were broader than mine. That same family turned up at the farm a few years later and wanted to buy Yumburra grain. Gabby reminded me that we had met before at the Cape Conran ceremony. She and her husband Chris run the Orbost brewing company, Sailors Grave, and they came to the farm to buy grain to make a beer they wanted to call Dark Emu. That coincidence was amazing enough but then I realised that I had taught Gabby's brother and sister at Mallacoota School in the seventies.

They asked me about my preferred style of beer and, being a bogan, I recommended a dark beer like Tooheys Old. They have made a very good beer and we get a small percentage from the sale of every slab. The money we receive has been spent to support Aboriginal students at Orbost High School and two in Sydney through the Goodes-O'Loughlin Foundation (GO Foundation). We are also sponsoring one of our own farm team to learn film making.

The huge reach of history from the turning of Chance's wheel is dramatic but it all began with Uncle Muns, the son of a little boy who survived the massacre. Only one child survived the incident and was reared by the family of the perpetrators, not an uncommon event on the frontier.

Despite those circumstances, Uncle Charlie Hammond was secretly instructed in lore by several old Aboriginal men. Uncle Charlie then passed that lore on to Uncle Muns who gave it in turn to Uncle Max and he gave it to us.

Uncle Max died just before Christmas 2021. Gurandgi had been with him only a couple of days before to perform a ceremony at Burnum Burnum Sanctuary park in Sydney. In preparation, Nathan and I got busy cutting bush poles so we could make a bower for his coffin. We stripped the inner golden bark off the poles and took it with us to the burial at Tilba Tilba, in the shadow of Gulaga Mountain. One of the lasting memories of my life will be the sight of ten Gurandgi sitting in a circle and weaving that bark into rope. As each few metres was finished, we used it to lash the poles together. All for you, Unc. Thank you.

Rope made from woven bark

We lost a huge mind and heart and we never expected that the gap would be painless, but even so, we were not fully prepared for the pain that overflowed during the rest of the year.

You're in a family too so you know how it goes. Add pain to undirected love, maybe some old trauma and a few grievances and the grief sprawls and corrodes. Unc left us a very specific plan for handling the earthquake and gradually the tremors abated but all of us have been shaken and hurt. Fortunately, that wise old man anticipated all of it and left a plan for the recovery too: love coupled to his old trinity of Patience, Tolerance and Respect. I call on them every day to check that I am truly following the lore he gave us. The lore is no mystery, it is almost always about decency.

In preparation for Uncle's ceremony, Gurandgi began collecting plants and ochres from all the Yuin lands and some were sent from distant communities where Uncle was remembered and revered.

Our son, Jack, was arriving by air from Apollo Bay for the ceremonies, so we had this rare family gathering in the midst of the turmoil. Jack has become king of the Gurandgi kitchen so, once he had landed, we collected food for Uncle Max's last camp. I drove on to Tilba to prepare the ceremony site and after assembling all the materials, the clay, leaves, poles, bark and firewood, I headed to Narooma where Lyn, Jack and I were staying in an eccentric little house on the Narooma foreshore.

You see so little of your children when they have their own families so Lyn and I soaked in the time we had with our son. All of us under the same roof once again.

I was up at dawn and went out to finish the bough shed and clad it with fresh greenery. Other Gurandgi were there preparing the ochres and some were getting the fungus and bark tinder ready for the smoking.

The day was long, involved and inevitably, in such a large group, where grief had frayed the nerves, there were some people at odds with each other and they tiptoed around, everyone doing their best to ease Unc's passage into his next life.

Once the ceremony started, we were bound in a structure that had every movement predetermined. My daughter, Marnie, arrived and I could see her and Lyn at the edge of the gathering, but it was many hours before I could get to them.

The ceremony proceeded on its inexorable path and the graciousness of it all was a balm. Galoo, a White-faced Heron, did a complete circle around us and, later, many of us mentioned having seen the slow progress of the bird.

That night Lyn, Jack and I had a meal in the noisiest restaurant I have ever been to, but in some ways, it was a relief. We were too tired to talk.

We returned to Gipsy and helped Lyn clean 'Riverbed', our bed and breakfast, before taking Jack back to the airport. Such a rush, so little time with our son. But grateful for what we had. Thanks once again, Unc.

When I got back to the farm there were three Wedgies in the duck yard. The drake, Quacky, was dead. Quacky was granddaughter Charlee's duck. It was 9 January, Charlee's birthday. I knew I couldn't tell her such news on her special day. It took me hours to clean up the mess amongst the traumatised ducks. Death upon death.

Dogs

I said I'd never mention boats again, but you didn't believe that, and it surprises me that it has taken so long to mention dogs. But we're still grieving.

In 2007 we were helping to build the CFA shed at Gipsy Point and the roof plumber volunteer, Jim, was coming all the way from Wroxham at the top of the Jinoor valley above Wangarabell. He had to bring his new litter of pups with him every day. Jim lived in an old house on one of the old farming properties in a district that went bust.

Perhaps he thought if he brought the pups he might sell some. He did.

Every smoko I sat on the sand heap with a cup of tea and the old bitch, tired from the tearing claws of eight fervent blue heelers, came and snuggled under my arm. Do something, she seemed to be saying.

We chose a very pretty, dappled girl and a big, dopey-looking boy whose geniality tugged at your heart. We called them Wangarabell, for the valley town closest to their birth place, and Yambulla for the mountain under which they were born.

They were living a life of wild dogs on that remote farm and their history is cautionary. One pup was taken by an eagle, another two were bitten by snakes, a different two were run over by their owners, one was lost to history, and Mum and Dad succumbed to old age, old Butterfly and Ozzie.

Just Wangarabell and Yambulla remained of that whole family. And we lost Yambulla just before Uncle Max passed. Bulla had gone blind and deaf but he would still race out into the middle of the paddock and throw himself down and squirm in the ecstasy only a dog on its back seems to know. He knew the paddock so he felt confident and safe, but then he started to lose balance and one morning his head was askew and he was staring up at the sun. He was very confused. My heart sank.

I'd had two difficult nights with him. On both nights he asked to be let out but I had to go with him because he was really disoriented. I followed my old friend around and around the farm. If I touched

Wangarabell and Yambulla

him he wagged his tail, if I spoke he smiled, but his life was a shambles and he knew it. I hated to see his indignity.

We have the world's best vet in this district, Wendy Mashado, and she had explained the head tilting phenomenon. Vets don't know why it happens but it always comes just before death. Wendy had also explained that she would be away for a week. I watched Bulla's perplexity as he stared up at the sun whose brightness must have been registering somewhere in a confused corner of his brain.

I dug a hole and got the gun. I had to help out my dear mate. He slumped neat as could be and trembled for a little before we buried him on his old cushion and planted a banksia above him. Lyn knew what was happening and had stood out of sight on the front verandah. Nathan arrived for work and saw Lyn, didn't say a word, and went and hugged her.

The Bidwell-Maap who stayed at Lyn's house for years used to call Yambulla and Wangarabell the Bidwell spirit dogs because of their names. We called them friends because of their nature.

Harvest

We grow the old Aboriginal grains and tubers at Yumburra for many reasons. They are perennial so they sequester carbon, they are soil

Murnong seed: Yam Daisy

builders, and they are more nutritious than their Western equivalents, but we also wish to make a political statement: these are our foods and we maintain cultural contact with them. But of all the money made from so-called 'native food' or 'bush tucker', terms we refuse to use, only 1 per cent goes to Aboriginal people.

If Australia wanted to make a real contribution to Aboriginal employment and prosperity, here is the opportunity. We are supported by a few philanthropic organisations but we need Australians to buy Aboriginal food from Aboriginal companies. That is why we started Black Duck Foods, to make a difference to Aboriginal communities and our economy.

It's hard work, as any farming operation is, but it brings our people into intimate contact with the land and our culture. The economic benefits flow through to our families where children see their parents work on something they love and the household is not dependent on

Ready for harvest at Yambulla

government, which is a spiritually enervating existence. We believe in the dignity of work.

Chris and Terry have been working hard at the Mallacoota Airport harvesting grain. The Shire have allowed us to harvest the airport for the last five years but gaining access is becoming harder as insurance premiums become more expensive and restrictive. We are sorry not to be able to harvest there in the future but the airport grain, and that harvested at Robert and Irene Allan's farm at Timbillica, enabled us to refine the processes required to achieve clean grain.

We are also very lucky to harvest various grains at Yambulla (near Wroxham) and Bendoc. The generosity of those farmers gives us an opportunity to learn more about our plants and how to train other Aboriginal communities in their use.

The tenth of January was such a day and we were helped by Peter Thompson who heard about the farm on a podcast and offered to help. He removed Madagascan Fireweed and thistles, both bad invaders of open country. He helped us harvest Murnong seed too and we were very grateful because volunteer labour is very useful in picking up the jobs we can't get around to during harvest time.

Later that day I went and fixed the bilge pump on *Nadgee* as there had been rain that week and I needed to empty her unless she sank again. Yes, another story, another book!

Snakes

A telltale shiver of grass exposed a black snake moving into the duck pen. The girls had had enough terror and excitement in their lives and they moved toward the intruder with their heads nodding. A duck is a peaceful and incompetent animal in many ways and Michael Leunig used them as conjurers of our better angels. Even so, the snake thought better of it and headed for the bean patch instead. No picking beans today!

The snakes on the property cause consternation in almost everyone who works and visits, but I have lived with them all my life and have never had any trouble.

Once on King Island as a child I grabbed a Tiger accidentally while climbing a riverbank, but all I got was a hiss and a stern look. I don't like having Tigers and Browns around the house, because the grandkids never look where they are going and those snakes are unforgiving. The beautiful Red-bellied Black Snake, however, is a gentle companion, so she is allowed free board.

The black snake is known to keep Tigers and Browns from its territory. If you have black snakes you are unlikely to have the others. The only black snake to turn on me was because I had just cut it in half. That benighted serpent was living in the woodshed at Cape Otway. None of us wanted to feel a thick and writhing body while gathering wood for our fire as we got to the bottom of the pile just around the start of spring.

That snake, or half of it, took deep offence and I regret it to this day. Like the cat we found at the Cape whose owner had hooked the cat's paw through its collar to stop it wandering. That cat wandered anyway and the hard plastic collar bit deep into its armpit and the infection was putrid.

It was a lovely, glossy black cat and had kept itself clean and fed while on the run, all but for the wound beneath its front leg. It came to the back door mewling for help. I picked it up, inspected the wound, smelt the corruption and calculated the numbers of Potoroos and Blue Wrens it had killed while on the loose.

She trusted me that cat, she was appealing to me, but I picked up the tomahawk and clipped her neatly on the back of the head. I regret that even though the septicemia would have been a far more horrible death. But we had looked into each other's faces. I regret it. It hurts me still. All the deaths of all the injured animals I have had to deal with in a country life have never left me.

Even the snakes. Terry was aghast when I killed the Tiger Snake in our Nullamaa (north) garden. But that is where our granddaughter Alia had been recklessly plunging her hand amongst the vegetables while hunting out strawberries that very morning.

We are two and a half hours from the nearest place that has anti-venom. Sorry Tiger Snake, sorry Terry, but Alia comes first.

Covid

We had been incredibly lucky with Covid. While the rest of the state was in lockdown, we were able to access shops because we lived inside what the authorities referred to as the 'border bubble'. Our workers could cross it because they were deemed essential agricultural employees.

We had two workers living on the farm, Chris and Lindsay, who had arrived as volunteers but proved so useful that they became employees and they stayed because life at the farm was better than the walls of a flat in Canberra or Newcastle.

We had dinners cooked on the campfire, we went fishing and played pool at the back of the local pub. Life was pretty good. And so much work got done because the rest of the world was shut down and there was nowhere to go.

In the second lockdown my daughter Marnie, husband Justin, and children Marlo, Alia and Charlee all stayed at the farm. Chris played extraordinary games with them, Lindsay taught them to ride his horses and Marnie homeschooled them. Unforgettable days.

I found the kids' table manners appalling but three months of my instruction reaped little result. Grumpy grandfather became my appellation. I still think knives and forks are a good thing and the sight of someone else's half-digested food is not. There!

But, once again, we got a lot done. Mundabaa, the local Aboriginal building company, built a bedroom and office for me and a workshop and nursery for the farm. But the distance from Eden and the new Covid restrictions made progress slow, so it made sense for the painting and fittings to be finished by Justin and Lindsay.

The four rooms were designed by Christy, the architect from Gipsy, but material shortages and travel restrictions meant we had to compromise Christy's aesthetic. I was away so much during the building that I needed Christy to manage the job. One day when we were standing in the lounge room contemplating the colour scheme, I told the story of George who started the farm and the separation from his wife and the onset of depression and his suicide in this very room, according to my neighbour.

We were considering the sorrow of mankind when our gazes drifted to the ceiling and stopped at an unusual small round hole. We fell silent.

It took ages for the spirit of the farm to settle when I took it over in May 2018. Many tricksters seemed to be at work around the place, but I lived in a caravan until a cricket mate, Dossi, finished painting and the new hardwood floor had been installed.

Even after that work was finished, I found many reasons not to sit in the lounge room. My entire lounge furnishings were a steel garden chair and a box for a coffee table. The dogs hated it and complained and grizzled because they didn't have a comfy chair. I relented after a year and bought an on-special lounge suite from Smith's in Pambula. They loved it and we could all snuggle on it in front of the fire. Peace at last.

Peter Ahmat, Torres Strait Island and Yorta Yorta man, and Bobby Maher, Yuin man, were the main builders and did a great job given the hardships and remoteness. Bobby's deck is a constant source of wonder to me and I am so grateful for his cleverness in managing all the angles and levels required to match the new building with the old and rickety.

Mundabaa also built the two 20 metre by 30 metre enclosed gardens, which are the heart of our tuber production. It was a hard build because of the sloping land but the result is a constant source of pride. We found a lot of stone tools when we dug the holes for the steel posts and an image of ten Aboriginal men gathered around an old chalcedony core will never leave me. How did that stone get here? Where did it come from? Which Yuin man carried it? Was it a relative?

The small axe head knapped from that stone must have been an incredibly beautiful object. Mauve, amber and pearl. You can imagine the whole community gathering around to admire it, just as we did, 150 years later. That stone, along with others found around the house, are still on a bench on the verandah. I show it to everyone who has five minutes to spare. We are not dead and neither is our history of art and labour!

Justin is very handy on the tools and plugged away during Covid, and finally I could sleep in my own room. The family could have the old farmhouse to themselves and I could make a cup of tea in the early morning without upsetting the whole apple cart.

Harvests and Cuckoos

The Channel-billed Cuckoo used to be a rare visitor, but it soon became a regular. I heard its call first in early spring but it was still here in late summer. The Scarlet Honeyeater used to be rare too, but climate change has made them common visitors. Muttonwood and Heart Plants used to also be uncommon but now find the warming climate to their liking.

The drizzly weather meant the fellas worked in the hayshed welding steel benches for the new nursery. Chris is a bit of a wizard when it comes to making things. A youth spent wrecking and repairing trail bikes means he looks at a job and can usually figure out a solution. He's a deeply cultural man and can repair any machine.

While they were working, I wrote an essay for *Indigenous Perspectives* and then Terry, Nathan and I had to go to Eden for the monthly Twofold Aboriginal Corporation. Twofold manages housing, health and some education for the community and battles hardship and disadvantage every day. The staff are superb. No one wants their job but they do heroic work for little pay. I admire them immensely. Many talk about Aboriginal disadvantage, some people try to end it.

During a quiet day on the farm, I provided myself the luxury of sitting on the verandah on my new second-hand bench and reading Sylvia Hallam's *Fire and Hearth* for the second time, just for the pleasure of it. I looked up from the book and wondered when I had last read a book for the sheer joy of it. The answer was thirty years ago.

Twenty of those were during our publishing and editing of *Australian Short Stories* magazine when we read 120 stories every week for nineteen years. It robbed me of the private pleasure of the book. I miss that luxury of spare time. Hallam talks about the agricultural organisation of Aboriginal people, so I suppose you could argue it was work anyway.

I let the book rest in my lap as I absorbed the luxury of reading and a moment of rest. There are so few moments to sit down and reflect that it allowed me time to be grateful. The word rest appears in the word restore.

In this moment of calm and reflection on language, I thought of Groucho Marx. I think Groucho constructed one of the world's best jokes. 'Outside of a dog a book is a man's best friend. Inside of a dog it's too dark to read.'

I analysed that joke with Julie Clarke a couple of years ago and her forensic knowledge of language and grammar brought the joke alive again. I thought of a time when we swam at Bronte watching children being taught to love water. We mused on children, water and hope. A poem from that day will appear in my collection of poetry, *Bronte Babes*.

It was restful considering these luxurious cul-de-sacs of thought on the new verandah, so thank you, once again, Bobby Maher, I think of you often with gratitude. Thank you to everyone who worked on these new rooms, I enjoy the fruit of your labour every day and every night. You have made a wonderful place. Thanks to Pete Ahmat too, because while he worked on the building, we spent hours poring over books of history and heritage and talking black politics.

The building took so long and was undertaken in such difficult times that I am conscious of all those who helped create this calm place, this haven.

While I read, the magpies warbled for the entire hour. Thank you Garramagang your company is appreciated, your soulful art understood.

Later in the week it was John Williams's funeral in Eden and it reminded us that time is precious. He was an influential Aboriginal man but is now gone. The Eden community has been wracked by too many funerals recently, very sadly many of those were for young people.

And speaking of precious time, Lyn worked with our ninety-three-year-old Gipsy neighbour as they wrangled an insurance claim after Pat hit a kangaroo. The roo lived but the Subaru was cactus. Pat has been such a good friend and a great supporter of Aboriginal people.

March is the season of fruit and so, in the midst of cooling preserve jars, I began writing a kids' novel about ducks and eagles. I lost the manuscript for a while but eventually found it under a pile of tractor repair bills. I called the story *Ducks and Drakes*.

The garden hits its straps around that time of the year and I harvested tomatoes, cucumbers, plums, lemons and Vanilla Lilies. I will make cordial from the lemons and chutney and stewed fruit from the plums. The kitchen will smell of boiling fruit for a week but right through the next nine months I will have the flavours of plums, apples and rhubarb on my cereal every day. Never forget the bounty of Mother Earth.

Lyn made a loaf of bread for the Twofold Aboriginal Corporation AGM. The memory of the first loaf made about seven years ago remains sentinel in my mind. Bread made from our grains. When was the last time that had happened? The responsibility of closing that gap in history weighs heavily on us and I don't think a day goes by when someone on the farm doesn't refer to that duty.

We had early help from Ben Shewry (Attica Restaurant), John Reid (RedBeard bakery), Michael James (Tivoli Road Bakery), Richard Cornish (food writer for *The Age*) and Max Allen (wine writer), and many of them were in the kitchen when that first loaf came out of the oven. There were cheers and raised glasses so conscious were we of the history of the moment and what it could mean for Aboriginal communities and all Australians.

Sentiment and duty went out the window, however, as the bread was broken. It was superb. The aroma filled the kitchen. A handful of seed smells like a summer dusk; Australia will love cooking with this flour. Bakers will make a fortune from selling its wares, but how will Aboriginal people benefit? Some government minister, public servant or patriot will read this, so I plead with you to work out an answer to that question. Not just from your own brain and experience but after inquiring from Aboriginal people how they see the community's involvement. Sit across the table from us, break bread together, be equal.

Birran Durran Durran

I saw two young plovers on 15 January. Tiny beige fluffs with long legs. Slightly ridiculous. Despite their vigilance, the Spur-winged Plover loses a lot of chicks to eagles and foxes. I can't see how dingoes would have much success because the racket made by the adults when a dingo is within a kilometre breaks their cover immediately. Foxes are stealthier and patient and probably have success while eagles torment the birds with casual fly-bys seemingly aimed at wearing down the vigilance.

The plovers often nest right on the road at the big corner above the dam. I have seen three sets of eggs over the years, right in the median strip; dull green eggs camouflaged by the stones and grass where they are laid.

The birds feign injury and totter and stumble in front of the ute in an attempt to lure us away from the nest. They are probably encouraged in this manoeuvre because, in their opinion, we always fall for it. I have seen Australian Pipits do the same thing, but I have never found their nest, whereas a casual stroll will normally reveal the plover nest.

Their calls are ever-present on the farm. If the horses gallop, an eagle passes, a dingo wakes or a car arrives, you hear about it instantly. You can't make friends with Birran Durran Durran because everything is a threat in its opinion. The helmeted yellow face gives the bird an appearance of suspicion. I love them but they do not love me.

If I shoot at starlings they go berserk. Starlings have tried to set up a colony on the farm every year at the beginning of spring and so I take pot shots at them with my ancient Lithgow .22 rifle.

I rarely hit one, but the report of the gun has the horses plunge into a gallop at the first sound. Every bird seems to react too. You can slam a car door or drop a steel saucepan or bucket and they don't even look up. What is it about the rifle report that causes such immediate consternation?

Camouflaged plover's eggs

The Spur-winged Plover

Many Australian bird names reference military regalia: riflebirds, Albert's Lyrebird, frigatebirds to name a few. But the plover with that masked face and distinctive tan, black and white is not one of them. I think they are a vastly underrated bird for character and appearance. They are so neat and so stiff in their bearing.

I am still trying to find out the meaning of their name, Birran Durran Durran. I keep wondering if it means stop-start. The birds often dash stiff-legged for a few metres and stop suddenly as if in a game of musical chairs where the prize is greater than a Mintie.

One of Uncle Max's many names was Dulumunmun (short legs). One of his totems was the Red-capped Dotterel (plover), a shore bird that also runs in fits and starts. It's funny, but I never thought of Uncle Max as a short man because I was always looking up to him.

The plover alarm raised when the eagles invaded the duck pen must have been dramatic, but no one could help these helplessly domesticated birds. They might tilt their head toward the sky in search of prey but they are no match for it. Even if you steal eggs from beneath a sitting duck, the tap from her beak is like she's testing your reflexes rather than trying to hurt you.

They had been so intimidated and traumatised by the avian attacks that they barely left the hutch, but when I went in to mow their grass they followed me everywhere despite the noise, as if there was safety in numbers.

Gamelan

A rainy period inspired the frogs. The nights were full of riot and every now and then the low honk of a swan lent an air of Balinese gamelan to the orchestra. The plovers' voices interceded on a need-to-know basis and when the sun began to rise the butcherbirds and magpies took over. I don't have a sound system in the house because I'm so tuned in to what the rest of the farm family are saying. I don't want to miss any of it.

Lyn used to teach dance and she was meticulous in her search for the right music. One night a few winters ago I rowed her into the very end of the backwater where a flock of swans had their own gamelan underway. It was entrancing. We recorded it and we had planned to use it in a performance on the sandflats in Mallacoota's Bottom Lake. The idea was to acknowledge the fact that the place has been Aboriginal land and always would be, but the hope was that all residents could live together here in peace. Because the only other option is denial and argument.

There is a map of Mallacoota's lakes drawn by the government surveyor Francis Peter MacCabe in 1847, soon after the first entry of Europeans into the district. All place names on it are Yuin words so MacCabe must have been accompanied by an Aboriginal guide. I have often wondered if it was Mallacoota Kitty who was later murdered, by repute, by Captain Stevenson after whom the location of Mallacoota's first white settlement was named.

Locals told me in the seventies that Mallacoota did not have an Aboriginal population. This map should dissuade anyone from that view. A copy of the map was found by Russel Mullet being used as a drawer liner in the Lands Department. Russell gave it to me and later I found the original map thanks to a friend of Chris Solazzini, one of the farm workers. I copied it and had it mounted and framed and tried to give it to the East Gippsland Shire Council.

I could tell there was some resistance when they asked me about the map's authenticity. Apart from the fact that it is clearly produced by a government surveyor, anyone wanting to find it could discover its bona fides in the government records office.

It wearies me that we have to argue these things to the very death with government officials. It's also true that some local Aboriginal people want to argue the toss on the language, who owns the land and what that land is called, but these arguments arise in an atmosphere where groups compete for far too little money and influence. The legacy of colonisation. People who despise Aboriginal people and who want Australia to remain a white colony love any sniff of division and use it as a mallet to squash the opinion of those who have more diplomatic and generous opinions.

It was only in the 1960s that *The Bulletin*, Australia's most popular magazine for 130 years, dropped the masthead, 'Australia for the White Man'.

Mallacoota should celebrate the map that proves black people lived in this paradise, but it has been a long and depressing saga. Eventually the Mallacoota Bunker Museum took possession of the map, ironically, in a building administered by the Shire.

We should be using names on that map too. The lakes have been imaginatively named by Europeans Top and Bottom, the islands,

Rabbit, Horse and Goat! The map shows the real names of those islands and a name near the entrance is Mallacoota. Mallacoota means white pipeclay which erupts at several points on the lake and is still collected ritually and used in cultural ceremonies today.

When the groups with cultural authority come together one day, I hope we can use our voice to replace the insult of Rabbit, Horse, Goat, Top and Bottom. It would allow us to celebrate the land and agree to share it because sharing is the only way; neither black nor white is going away.

While the weather was cool Lyn covered bunches of grapes with little socks to keep the bowerbirds, possums and honeyeaters away, but looking out the bedroom window one night I saw a Brush-tailed Possum (Goomera) enjoying a bunch on top of the Muslim Gate, for all the world like Bacchus.

The Muslim Gate was built to stop the Garragagan (west wind) burning the tree ferns poking through the deck. I bought the grills and doors separately from Jason and Sylvie at Maggie and Rosie's Antique Emporium in Bega. That store is a solace for me. After the building got close to being finished there was little left for furniture but I found wonderful things in Jason's Aladdin's den. I furnished the house for much less and more to my taste than buying new.

I have a little writing bureau in my bedroom which has about forty tiny drawers where I put all the bits and pieces that come out of my pocket at night. Coins, screws and washers, fishing hooks and sinkers, bullets, shells and stones. I reckon there are over 200 dovetail joints in the desk. It would be impossible to pay someone to make a desk like that today.

Furniture from Maggie and Rosie's Antique Emporium

I love putting my hand on it, the wood is like silk, but I pity whoever has to clean up my room when I'm gone. Suck it up, there's sure to be something worth saving. I cleaned up for my parents and in-laws, so I'm setting land mines for my own kids. Set aside a week, you mob!

When I brought the doors home Lindsay was too scornful to mock. He was silent while I scraped them back and gave them a rough paint with the dark blue of the house trim. I could feel his eyes judging me as I smashed out the awful yellow bubble glass in the screens so that the grills could stand out.

Whoever previously owned the gates had pasted Koranic verses all over them and there were two peepholes and several chains and locks. I often wonder if Goomera finds the peepholes useful. Is there an owl on the other side? A fox? A grapevine?

I love coloured glass and have done so since I was a child. I loved looking through bottles at the transformed world. Seaglass was collected every day. Yes, there are dozens of pieces in the writing desk. I bought some faceted glass sphere in a second-hand shop in Blackheath and I stuck one on the top curve I had planed and fitted above the gates, but Goomera had it off in two days.

When the whole family collected for pre-Christmas at Warrnambool later in the year, I stopped at a second-hand shop in Terang and at the front door there was a crate of brass door furniture and coat hooks. Five bucks each, mate. I got some hinges, handles, drawer pulls and a few other things so mysterious their use is pure speculation. But they're lovely. A lovely brass doorknob is now on the top of the gate and is fixed with screws and it has defied Goomera's best efforts.

The Pombomart is a huge old butter factory and is held together by cobwebs and dust. It is a rambling mess of objects. After Terry, Lyn and I attended a whale festival conducted by the Couzens family in Warrnambool, I asked Terry and Lyn to choose items to remember our journey by.

Terry chose a wooden Mirrigan (dingo), Lyn a butter dish and I was delighted by my two Chinese lion bookends. They are really heavy for their size and I think they're wonderful on top of the old desk. Every time I look at them I think of Gurawul, the whale, and the families who asked us to join their celebration in Gunditjmara Country.

I wasn't to know it then but in 2023 we had a second whale ceremony at Apollo Bay with the Couzens family, Gurandgi and ninety other whale people from all over Australia. While we were dancing, a whale and her calf breached several times. Locals couldn't believe it, having never seen whales in that stretch of water before.

Bell interrogates the possum, Goomera

But back in 2022, when we were in Warrnambool for our Christmas gathering, I badgered everyone into going to the Fletcher Jones second-hand market and gave them orders to choose something. Marlo got some anime shirts, Alia got the best burgundy Mock Martins anyone has seen, Marnie a tea set in a wicker basket, which we have used three times on river picnics already. It lends itself to ceremony.

Lyn got a set of beautiful jugs, Jack and Shell have enough junk already, Justin was trying to preserve space in the car, Lily got some books, but Charlee chose a stuffed giraffe taller than herself. I could see Justin trying to interest her in smaller, more aesthetic objects, but true to her nature she declared it was the giraffe or nothing.

Laugh Ya Half Giraffe

That giraffe appears in every photo taken during the weeks leading up to Christmas. I wanted to call it Laugh Ya Half Giraffe but Charlee held firm on Amber. That family excursion and the hour spent on the Fletcher Jones lawns drinking coffee and eating toasted sandwiches touched me to the heart. You can never be sure that same collection of people will be in the sun together ever again. It's a treasure for me and I hope the family remember it. Writing about it also gave me the chance to write Laugh Ya Half Giraffe. The family just looked at me when I said it but my sense of humour cheers me even while it leaves others worried about my general stability.

Anyway, that's the story of the Muslim Gate. I wonder about the courtyard that it protected somewhere in Sydney but love the fact that it is now the gateway in the north to my fern-sheltered verandah and a view of the eagles' eyrie to the south. It doesn't matter that others think it strange, I think it's perfect.

Lyn has been watching this year's young eagle lumbering through the grass with inelegant plunges. I think the dunnarts are mocking it but that hapless bird will soon dominate the sky and has a spiritual legend to compare with any other creature on Earth. Lumber on creator spirit.

It was close to the hottest time of our year, the middle of January, and when I brought the boat back to the jetty, Koon ar rook (Wood Duck) was sitting on the jetty rail. I drifted in and it didn't move until the bow rail nudged the jetty and then it flustered into the water. As I approached it seemed to have its eyes open but clearly hadn't seen me. Do they have a second lid that screens their eye when asleep?

I don't know and don't really need to know, but I'm aware that experiences like this are rare and, at my age, may never be seen again. I had a swim up into the creek to celebrate my mortality.

Summer Flowers, Butcherbirds and Herons

Toward the end of summer, the Bloodwoods and Angophora flower in creamy clusters. Birds riot in the blossoms. The air is a squabble of sound with the background drone of bees and insects and I never fail to be reminded of Steve Wadsworth, an old teacher mate and bushwalker. When he died too early we picked armfuls of Bloodwood blossom for his funeral.

The butcherbird's call is clear and bell-like in autumn but in summer it has a more insistent tone. It was coming from the Grey Box trees on the bluff above the Yumburra Creek that feeds into the Wallagaraugh. These trees are remnants of the old forest and because of their size and the sparsity of brush beneath them they did not burn in the 2019-20 fires. Too big to burn, their first branches too far above the ground and their separation from each other too great to allow easy spread of fire. It is a lesson for Australian forestry that we can calm forest fire by allowing bigger trees to form these safe environmental zones.

We need timber but we don't need to waste it on wood pulp for hamburger wrappers. Bigger trees are safer but also provide the heart of the forest. At Gipsy Point groups of Ironbark trees on every ridge-top provide habitat for thousands of birds and marsupials. You cannot pass these trees in a boat without being impressed by the abundance of life in their branches. Beneath every one of these ridge groves are thousands of Aboriginal artefacts.

Please leave those old tools in place because they are records of our Old People's lives and in situ they are like the Mitchell or La Trobe libraries, stolen they are like the glimmering stone picked up from the tideline: once removed it is a lifeless semblance of itself and soon discarded in the button jar or tossed out in the rubbish. Leave vibrance to remain vibrant.

Galoo, the White-faced Heron, is more lugubrious than vibrant and its guttural call is often heard during these hot days. It sounds cross or judgemental, but it's the time for these elegant birds to fly ponderously about the riverbanks and paddocks in their ritualised mating.

The courting flights are long and languid and, like the egrets, they are stately birds who never seem in a hurry. They stand sentinel over favoured pools or pastures, erect and elegant. They object to any disturbance with harsh croaks and groans and stern glances. During Uncle Max's funeral at Tilba, one walked around the edge of the cleared area of the reserve in very precise steps, jabbing at the prey it found there at regular intervals. Because we couldn't move, that bird was more or less our timekeeper. Its progress around us metronomic. It is wise to observe these things and learn from them. Even if it's just about patience and acceptance.

Family

We have had a difficult twelve months defending Black Duck Foods from people unsympathetic to our Aboriginal employment policy. It made us wonder at the depth of cynicism within parts of the Australian heart. We were supported by an Aboriginal legal company whom we will never forget, but it was our board who stood strong and united.

Noel and Trish Butler, two members from our board, were superb in this fight for decency and Aboriginal inclusion, but they did so in a year when they were still recovering from losing their house to the fires. Noel lost all his family's artefacts too and both Noel and Trish lost their own artwork. They were devastated but hung tough for all our sakes.

We helped with some replanting and other things after the fires but this time we went up there just to thank them for their commitment to Aboriginal justice. The wider family has suffered the unbelievable pain of losing young members of the family in the last few months. This is common in Aboriginal communities and has its roots in the dispossession after the invasion of Australia but, more so, in the deeply institutionalised penalties and disadvantages for being black.

I was worried about them but when we arrived the place was full of family, bright young children and the latest babies. Young people were collecting wood for a ceremonial fire, there was cooking in the kitchen, laughter everywhere. That family looks after other families all the time, including Uncle Pirate, who deserves his own book. Pirate has lost a leg and an eye during his vivid life but remains a very complete character.

It was a long journey home but a beautiful drive along the coast.

When we returned, Terry and I were fixing some administrative details in the office and he noticed I had a manuscript for a story on Mallacoota Kitty, one of the few survivors of the Mallacoota massacres. 'That story has to be told, eh,' he said. Terry's old, old uncles and grandfathers walked the Jinoor valley trails in the 1860s and were familiar with that horrible story. Noel tells similar stories of his family. There is no getting away from it. The grief is ever-present. Aboriginal people deal with it every day.

Smoke

One of the great pleasures of the river is to take a slow trip to Gipsy. That's when you can surprise Water Dragons and Mirridar

(Sea Eagle). I don't get the time very often but there's an even more beautiful journey on that river system: a trip into Mallacoota for coffee or lunch. The voyage downstream and through the lakes is one of the great journeys of the world. I love taking Cousin Noel and Trish on that trip because their enthrallment makes it so special.

The journey has changed for me since the 2019 Black Summer fires, as so much has. My sense of smell has changed. I constantly smell smoke in the air, on my clothes, on the night air. The unbridled pleasure I used to take in the forest, waters and shores is now tinged with sadness and dread.

One of the people who remained fighting the fires on the river was Bart Brackley, a wild lad of the district. When I cut my way into the farm on that terrible day, the first person I saw was Bart trying to start

A journey on the river allows for special ceremony

a pump on the bridge. He was exhausted. He told me he hadn't slept for two days and his hands were trembling with weariness.

'Bart,' I said, in my best schoolteacher voice, 'go to bed and drink some water.' It must have sounded like good advice because that's what he did. I had taught his father and his aunty and uncles. Bart's grandmother, Maree, was a terrific woman and Bart had saved her house and that of his uncles and aunt. It was a heroic effort.

I taught most of the people who live on the river. We were an isolated community trying to get an education in one of the most remote places in Victoria. The Education Department had to be convinced that anyone could live so far from Melbourne. We did and we worked together. Last Christmas we reminisced in the Genoa pub about the extraordinary number of Mallacoota kids who won apprentice of the year in their various trades.

So, seeing Bart alone on the bridge I was not really surprised. He's a tough little bush nut, handy in a crisis. Bart told me that he was taking his 12-foot tinny into Mallacoota every second day to get fuel and supplies. The only time he really got scared was when the swag he keeps in the bottom of his boat caught fire.

My neighbours, the McLeods, yeah, I taught Darren and his brothers and sisters too, spent the night of the fire watching dead birds fall out of the sky as they anchored in the wide reaches of Bottom Lake. Darren was deeply upset by the lost birds but the soundtrack for it was gas bottles exploding in Mallacoota.

Another of the town's larrikins, Chad, is as wild as Bart but people in Terra Nova Drive reckon he saved half a dozen houses on his own. It's unfair to pick out individuals but I think the larrikins deserve a bit of good press every now and then.

I was in the CFA, so the day after the fires began I got the *Nadgee* and headed into town. I still had phone reception so I knew that a navy vessel was trying to evacuate people. I sailed the lake system as carefully as I could but the smoke was so thick and the landscape so changed I got lost crossing the Top Lake. Lost on my own river, I was disgusted.

I ended up in a little bay that was unrecognisable because every tree was burnt to the ground. I ducked and weaved in and out of a few more creeks and bays before I found the Narrows, which connect the two lakes. And I wouldn't have recognised it because its beacon was gone but the rock formation at its entrance is unmistakable.

I crept through the Narrows trying to stick to the centre of the channel but when I emerged into the Top Lake I could only see a few metres in front of me. I inched my way hoping to find the John Bull beacon in its centre.

I brushed past a green beacon pile and realised I was too far east and had to tack a little to the west, and at last I found the Bull and got around it into Mallacoota's navigation channel.

I couldn't see the town yet, but worse still, I couldn't hear it. There was not one other boat on the water, no vehicles, no voices, no birds. Total silence. The town seemed reduced, black gaps in every street. I moored the boat and walked up into town and got on a CFA Slip-On (an ultra-light fire tanker) with Les Barnes and went to Bastion Point to help with the unloading of fuel and the embarkation of the homeless.

There were friends of mine amongst the crowd trying to assist the naval officers but it was almost done in mime. Few people wanted to speak. They were in shock. It looked like a refugee column. The dogs were silent, benumbed, the cats in a trance. People held the pets in their arms seemingly unable to let them go.

After I left, Barnsey and I tried to get fuel for the farms upriver but it was hard. The town was short of fuel, everybody was desperate for it. I managed to fill my jerry cans and buy whatever I could from the store.

I sat for a moment and had a cup of coffee and a steak sandwich at Cafe 54. I had tears in my eyes, but it was unnoticed in the town that day. The redoubtable Tracey Hargreaves kept her store open to feed people and it was the best coffee I've ever had. I was so choked with gratitude I could barely speak to Tracey, yeah, I taught her husband, so we just nodded to each other. People got medals after that fire, but my hero was Tracey and her staff for providing five minutes of normality and peace. Thanks, mate, it kept me going.

Another one who never got mentioned was Lyn. She did the comms job at the CFA shed for a week. On the first day she heard a noise and turned around and the shed was on fire. A city brigade went and stood in front of that fire with their hoses on the fog setting. And saved the shed and survived. Lyn turned back to her computer. 'Yes, roger that, Tarneit, but I'm afraid we have no other tanker to support you at this stage.'

Her voice never varied as she passed out bad news to those stranded by the fire. People remember that voice and how the steady and clear instruction calmed them, even though it's not what they wanted to hear. Lyn set up the whole communication network, she was there at the start and still there at the end. Thanks to you too, mate.

Visitors to Mallacoota and Genoa tell of their horror at seeing the country after the fires. Grace McKenzie has been making a film about the farm and the aim to employ Aboriginal people within the culture. She first came at the end of the fires and was shocked at the devastation. She turned up again late in January 2022, but I don't think it was much improved from the first time. A leafless forest strikes at the heart of life.

I need to apologise to Grace because my enthusiasm for the film was very low. So much has happened, so much needs still to be done, the demands of the culture are so deep and, in many cases, not for display. There have been some big, very filmic moments, but the stakes were too high; the culture and people's wellbeing too fragile to expose to film. I know it frustrated Grace but there are some stories I'll never be able to tell outside the community.

Yambulla

The owner of Yambulla station, two hours north of here, saw a mention of my dog of the same name and was determined to meet us. Jim Osborne is a very generous man and, after that meeting, he was happy for us to harvest his Buru Ngalluk (Kangaroo Grass).

Those hot days brought the grain to ripeness, so we were flat out. Chris and Terry in their element out there, happy at the prospect of a good harvest.

Terry's family are the keepers of that valley's dog story.

The land is a more or less circular compound surrounded by a ring of mountains. These are the dogs. Mirrigan. One of the mountains is called Mirragunegin, place of the dogs. We are yet to get permission to tell the whole of that story, but it is coming.

Meanwhile, back at the farm, Nathan was working to bring a section of forest back to how it might have looked 150 years ago. This is a seventy-year program to fell smaller trees and encourage the maturity of others and the grasses that will grow beneath them once the canopy has been reduced. We know what that old pre-contact forest looked like in this area; graziers, missionaries, surveyors all described it in detail. Although fire had been used to maintain its structure, it actually resisted wildfire and made life safer and more comfortable for the Old People.

In the process of felling trees, we strip the poles of bark to use in construction jobs and we use the bark to make rope. Nathan made some beautiful lengths from these barks and we used some of them

Terry

for Unc's bower, but others will be used to join branches of a tree into a ring, a symbol the Old People used extensively.

We try to maintain the old traditions, and tree manipulation was a common forest language. It is my ambition to write a book about the altered trees around Australia so that they can be protected from accident and malice.

The farm doesn't work on Invasion Day. Normally I hide if I'm not at a community ceremony, but Grace wanted to film the boat trip into Coota so we sailed through the lakes under the supervision of Mirrigar (Sea Eagle). It was Lyn's first time in a boat since the rescue boat trips with the CFA and Fisheries during the fires so it was a solemn journey. The trip changed for us, so we weren't terrific company for Grace's purposes. We've been changed by the fire like much of south-east Australia. It's unavoidable. We can't help it.

On this day we learnt that Gurandgi Dean Kelly was back in hospital and seriously ill with Covid. He was in the same ward as the one where Uncle Max passed. Yes, a lot has changed in the last couple of years.

Life's Rich Tapestry, or Threadbare Carpet?

Nathan and Rochelle were getting married so I went up to Jigamy to mow the site and rake the buna ground. Raking the ground was restful, contemplative work and allowed me to return home rested where I set to work on the Mallacoota Kitty manuscript which I began in 2018 but lost.

It was a turbulent time as the reverberations from Uncle Max's passing opened old wounds in Uncle's family. Gurandgi have been trying to stand back from this aspect of the grieving but more and more we are being dragged into it to help settle disputes. This pain and suffering is inevitable but it is absorbing so much of our time and emotional energy.

I woke one morning very conscious of injured spirits and aware that something happened on the farm last night. Not a kangaroo in sight, very few birds calling. A visit from the dingoes?

A few days prior we had noticed the ravens arrive en masse. They seem to come with the maturity of the grasses. We thought they were Forest Ravens but a friend thinks they are Little Ravens.

We noticed the same thing twenty years ago at Cape Otway. One day there are none and next there is a cacophony of them all talking and interrupting each other. They are said to fly in from Tasmania and when they arrived at Yumburra there was such a prolonged and raucous conversation from eighty or so birds as if they had just arrived and were commenting on the Bass Strait crossing. Soon they were relatively quiet and feeding in the paddocks.

I was still fielding calls about Uncle Max's ashes. The pain is seeping into everything we do.

As an antidote to that, Jonathan Jones (Wiradjuri artist) and his partner Jen arrived to talk over big plans for a grass and cultural burning installation. They are a delight to have in the house. I think Jonathan is one of the most unusual people I know. He is such a daggy ratbag but there is no one more passionate about his culture. I love him to pieces.

After one exhibition on yam daisies and colonisation he gave me one of his delicately forged yams, which I treasure.

His new exhibition concentrates on artefacts and he has promised me one of the old shovels he made as a replica of ones found at the beginning of the invasion. Wouldn't it be wonderful if all Australians knew that Aboriginal people made shovels? Jonathan is leading the way.

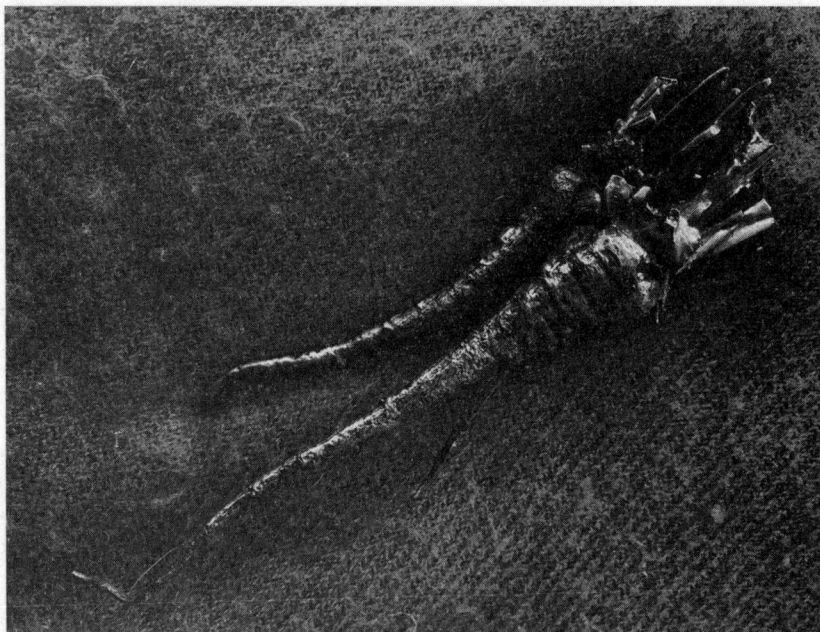

Jonathan's gift of a delicately forged yam tuber

He spends a lot of time with Uncle Stan Grant who has been very unwell. Jonathan is such a caring person. I am grateful to him for his care of Uncle Stan because I will never be able to repay the debt I have to Unc. That old man gave me crucial information about my mother's family. Details and contacts; it was such a wonderful gift. And he did that at risk of exposing himself to the baying hounds of the right-wing journalists who purport to know everything about the family of a man they have never met.

That episode of personal attack is still painful, but elders around Australia who either knew my family in those early years, or simply wanted to offer support, are sacred in my mind. Uncle Jim Berg, who has his own community issues, has been wonderful. When the media got stuck into me Jim sent me a parcel of artefacts including a stone from his Gunditjmara Country to show his support and keep me safe. I treasure that stone, Unc, and I have it in my pocket every day. It hasn't stopped the right-wing haters, but it has stopped me absorbing their hate. So grateful, I will never remind anyone how you pinged your hammy in the first fifteen seconds of a Koori carnival game at Kardinia Park in the eighties.

I don't know why people laugh when that happens but we did. It stopped the game but it is the only thing I remember about the day. Jim was a sporting legend for us all and so the irony of the ungracious and total collapse stopped us all in our tracks. It was Jim's knowledge of the boxing tent days which gave me access to some people with memories of my great-grandmother's family. Thanks, Uncle, and sorry for laughing. It was our love that made us do it.

Anyway, Derek Kickett came on and dominated. It was a revelation to see him move around tacklers so effortlessly. Derek was a big lad when he played for Essendon and Sydney in the AFL but he was a lot bigger by the time we saw him at Kardinia Park. Kardinia or Kardineu, rays of the early morning sun. What a beautiful name for a footy ground, how sad it is that the ground now has the inspirational title of GMHBA.

Our sporting ovals are now named after businesses which come and go. One year it's a car manufacturer and next it is a health fund providing health care to the rich. It must make clubs a lot of money to give up a name so evocative of Australia as Kardinia. The new ground in Melbourne used to be called Docklands, a perfectly suitable name as it is situated right in Melbourne's Docklands, but since then it has had a dozen names and the current one is Marvel Stadium, named after a comic book company, yes, quite appropriate.

And speaking of fleeting appearances, a few days after the Little Ravens arrived we found a flurry of delft blue Hairstreak Butterflies

Hairstreak Butterfly

on a group of wattles up near the Phoenix (resurrected from the fires) shed. In the wattles we had pupae, eggs and caterpillars. The first hatched males fluttered about the trees waiting for the females to emerge. The whole zoo was attended by Iridomyrmex Ants. In the one stringy little black wattle was a whole universe of activity.

Jonathon and Jen came and had a wonderful visit and the day they left I went for a swim and caught a beautiful bream on the bank opposite

Pelican Point near Gipsy. It is one of many favourite fishing spots, not least because it is beneath the giant Grey Boxes where the Whistling Kites nest. These birds are constant presences and at the nest their behaviour is a fascination.

The bream cooked beautifully in foil with just a little lemon juice, salt and pepper and butter. The simpler you cook fish the better. The juice and butter from the fish is an elixir.

One year we catered for a very flash dinner with Noel and Trish. Noel cooked his oysters on a grill above a campfire and, as they opened, we lifted the bottom half of the shell and squeezed lemon juice and myrtle into the cup of the top half.

They were a sensation and so many people came up to rave about them, most never having eaten an oyster hot.

Oyster is one of my totems and I'm not allowed to eat them unless served by a senior Yuin man. Cousin Noel kept me supplied, such a luxury. Uncle knew what he was doing when he gave me oyster. He knew I was an avid fisher and collector and must have thought prohibition wouldn't do me any harm. It hasn't. My enjoyment of oysters has been elevated by the rarity of their consumption. I look forward to senior Yuin men arriving; they always bring oysters.

The totemic system is not an opportunity to bequeath names, it is a responsibility. You are denied a food or object to remind you that your responsibility is to ensure the health and future of the totem. It is an environmental and spiritual sanction.

Just before he passed Uncle said to me, 'you can come off oysters now if you like', but I declined because I knew that my son, Jack, was about to qualify as someone who could serve them to me. I wanted to reserve and celebrate that rite of passage. Two dozen will be sufficient thank you, son. Wapengo Oysters if you can. And a Boag's or two.

The Hot Days of Early February

It is now the season of long hot days. The Yellow-rumped Thornbill was in the bottlebrush outside the kitchen window. They nest there most years but were absent last year so their arrival with their sweet song was so welcome. They'd been around the house for a week or so but were now into nesting behaviour. Their high splintery call is a charm to have close to the house. Another rare visitor is the Musk Lorikeet. I sometimes hear them down in the river Grey Boxes and their call is like two bits of broken glass being rubbed together. Rainbow Lorikeets are here every day and the raucous screeches are common but when a Musk flies by the difference in call is remarkable. I never fail to look up and greet them.

The pain in Uncle Max's family continues and bleeds into Gurandgi. Everyone is trying to manage it but all with different methods. Did we expect such a large gap would be filled easily?

Three Bunjil cruised over the duck pen again and the young one was calling its greedy little call. I had to check that the duck pen netting remains secure. I had a swim off the jetty to calm the nerves generated by the hungry screech. I feel for the ducks every time I hear it, but also for the parents for whom the call is designed. The crying baby.

The next day brought cricket training and that was enough to convince me that this would be my last game. The right arm no longer rotates smoothly enough for me to control the ball. Being able to move the ball and land it on a length has ensured me a game of cricket for as long as I can remember, but it is over. I feel very sad. People who don't play sport may scoff, but Saturdays were my day off. When I gave up footy at fifty-five my whole appreciation of the game changed. I am not a spectator.

I was an ordinary player and ordinary coach but I loved playing every one of my 520 games and really enjoyed those first couple of beers after the match immersed in the could-haves, might-haves and laughter of my mates.

After I retired I tried to watch games but the beer tasted terrible. I fear it will be true of cricket retirement. It's been a big part of my life and now it's over. The only chance every week to laugh and run around like a lunatic and scream out. It's not something you can do in the street.

Stones and Homes

Damo Coulthard and Rebecca Sullivan from Warndu Foods in South Australia came to the farm to talk over Aboriginal food production and how we can increase the Aboriginal share of the market beyond 1 per cent. It is an alarming statistic and makes a mockery of the feel-good acceptance of Aboriginal foods when that percentage indicates that it is just one more cultural dispossession. You can't eat our food if you can't swallow our history.

While we went back and forth from the gardens to the kitchen, I noticed that Damo was interested in an old grinding stone I had on the verandah.

Someone had dropped into the farm two years ago and said he had something for me. It was a pretty typical day with a busy work program underway and a couple of other visitors wanting to talk Aboriginal food, so I was a bit distracted, and the fella left the stone and disappeared before I could get his name and where the stone came from.

By chance, I met a friend of that fella in Bermagui one day and he said he could get the coordinates and a map of where the stone had

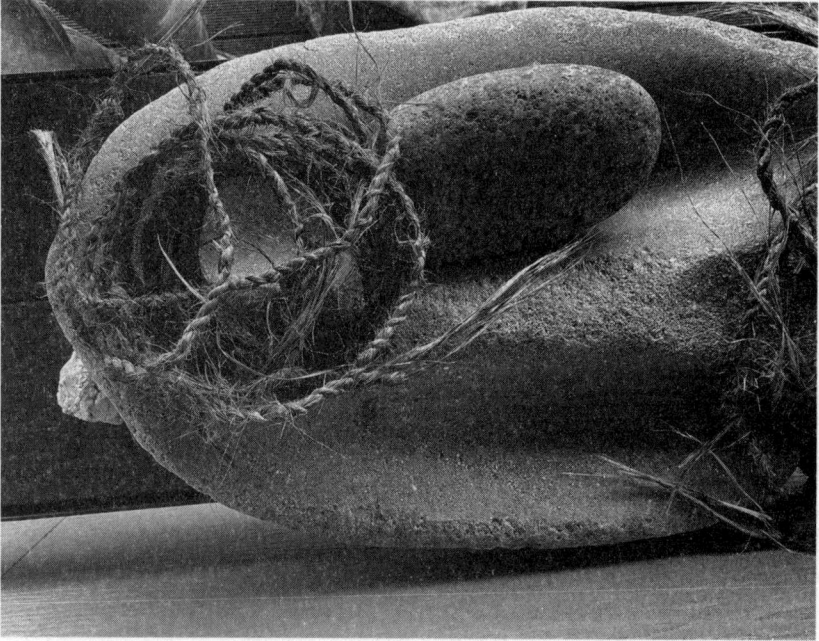

Grinding stone from Damien's Country

been found. What are the chances? Anyway, I said to Damo that I had noticed his interest in the stone and told him it had come from Innamincka. 'That's my Dieri Country,' he said.

The stone had been found on the edge of a river and taken to Queensland and suddenly the person with the stone must have got windy about it, decided he needed to get rid of it and brought it to Victoria. Just dumped it on me. I spoke to Uncle Max about it and we came up with a way of caring for the stone; we put it on Mum's old chair.

Damo rang his Uncle Cliff and they discussed the problem and decided that the stone could be repatriated to its right Country. The people have invited me to attend the repatriation ceremony when it is arranged. I'm really looking forward to that day because the stone comes from the Country where Charles Sturt had his life saved in 1845 by people north of Innamincka.

It was a remarkable moment in Australian history. The people had been harvesting grain in the ephemeral riverbed of Cooper Creek. That fact has huge significance for our country but was largely ignored by historians because of the assumptions needed to support the colonial invasion; that is, Aboriginal people were making no use of the land.

North of Cooper Creek at a site near Birdsville, archaeologists working with Josh Gorringe and Michael Westaway revealed this year that grinding stone blanks were mined at a number of locations on Mithaka Country. Scientists estimate that almost 3 million stones were removed and ground into dishes for grain processing. The scientists also estimated that those people only needed 1500 stones for their own use over the period when the mines were active. That is before the land was taken from the Mithaka people.

The rest of the stones were traded with other people. The next part of the investigation will be to find out how far afield the Mithaka stones were spread. Not for the satisfaction of Western enquiry but to learn about those cultural and trade links and how this whole network was conducted with such success and peace. The world is waiting for news of how trade can be undertaken without wars and without the creation of both billionaires and slaves.

A slab of stone, but a meaning with huge significance for humankind.

I sat on the verandah that night thinking about the relief of being able to send the stone on to its true Country. We smoked it well with fungus before it left. There's an important lesson in this for Australia, these objects were not abandoned; rather the owners were killed or dispossessed. The stones are markers of Australian history and culture and should be left where they are found.

Enjoy the exhilaration of being close to the oldest civilisation on Earth but to remove artefacts destroys the opportunity for the owners' descendants, and other Australians, the chance to find that connection to Country and people and stand for a moment contemplating the human journey.

I was drinking a can of Dark Emu, thanks to Gab and Chris at Sailors Grave Brewing, and I sat back as Googoonyellas (kookaburras) gave the longest recital of their rollicking song that I can ever remember. An extraordinary sunset and the frogs expressed their appreciation.

I recognised Peron's Tree Frog, Striped Marsh Frog, Brown Tree Frog and Whistling Tree Frog thanks to the FrogId app. Some say it's not important to know creatures by name, but I like to dignify all things by acknowledging their individuality and, in time, I hope we can recover the language names for each. Knowing the name builds relationship, one of the fundamental bonds between us all.

On Saturday 5 February, I stewed some tomatoes, and then went to an old mate's funeral. Sue Chapman was an iconoclast and an exceptional intellect. I will miss her deeply. As a kind of irony, she used to make the cricket team cucumber sandwiches for every home game. I had to train the lads in the knowledge that green stuff can be food.

Sue's ceremony was conducted at Bastion Point in light drizzle, but nobody flinched. Duncan Findlay, great town raconteur and ordinary cricketer, told remarkable stories of her life and a friend sang 'La Vie en rose' with deep passion. Just as well it was drizzling. We could wipe our faces with discretion.

I left Sue's memorial and went to the cricket ground very conscious of this being the last time I would play. We kept Tathra to ninety-two. We love beating Tathra so our batting performance had to be up to scratch. We beat them in the 2009 grand final and as I was captain, I treasure that memory and the photograph of Lyn laughing at our boyish pride.

We got the runs easily and young Ben Severs made a solid twenty-two to help get us there. His uncle is the publican and postmaster at Genoa. Everybody has to multitask in this district. I did nothing remarkable except stay alive and not hurt my shoulder. I enjoyed the beers and yarns afterwards in the new clubrooms while knowing I'd never again be part of the action.

I've played a lot of cricket and football on this ground graced by the giant Mallacoota Gum (*Eucalyptus globulus psuedoglobulus x cypellocarpa*). The memories are rich and many but this was the first time I had played there with the new clubrooms completed. Presto, team captain and nuisance, has a way of twisting official arms, and this new building is the product of his diplomatic insistence.

Grace wanted to do more filming so I told her the story of the mountains and valleys of the Australian Alps that I was told at the 150th anniversary at the Wave Hill Walk-off in 2016 at Daguragu. David Claudie, from Kuuku Ya'u Country in north Cape York, watched me for several days before calling me over to tell me a story 'about your south Country there'.

He drew the whole story and the landforms in the sand. He was meticulous about the shapes and the telling of the legend. I asked him when he had last been to the alps.

'I never been there, my old grandfather told me this story and he never been there either. We just know that Country. That is the story.'

If we ever needed proof of the close relationships built by the old storytracks that was the moment.

David is from the country where my white relatives on my father's side ended up. Pascoe River near Lockhart River. Maybe that's why he took his time watching me. I was aware of his gaze but didn't know why I was the subject of it.

Similarly, Uncle Max told a story his grandfather, Uncle Muns, told him when he was eleven. Uncle Muns had brought Uncle's old teachers, the Noble brothers, and the story was drawn in the sand on a roadside near Cathcart, NSW. The old men drew a figure and asked him to remember it before scrubbing it out and telling him he had to find the site of the original drawing during his lifetime.

Seventy-two years later he found it near St Helens in Tasmania. None of his old teachers had ever been to Tasmania but the strength of the storytracks ensured they knew how to draw it exactly. That story was at least as old as the submersion of the land below Bass Strait, 10,000 years ago.

It was the story of Gurawul, the whale, and how he saved the people from drowning. Go west, he told them, climb to higher ground. You will meet fellow Aboriginal people there and you will be asking them to share their land. So be polite, be respectful, do not fight for land.

The sharing was done, probably not without hardship, but was conducted, as Gurawul had asked, in peace. Yuin Gurandgi live by that lore today.

After filming that pattern with Grace, I spent the next day dealing with a management dispute. It is so disappointing that 230 years after the Invasion, Aboriginal people still have to defend their culture every day.

But it has to be done or colonial myth prevails.

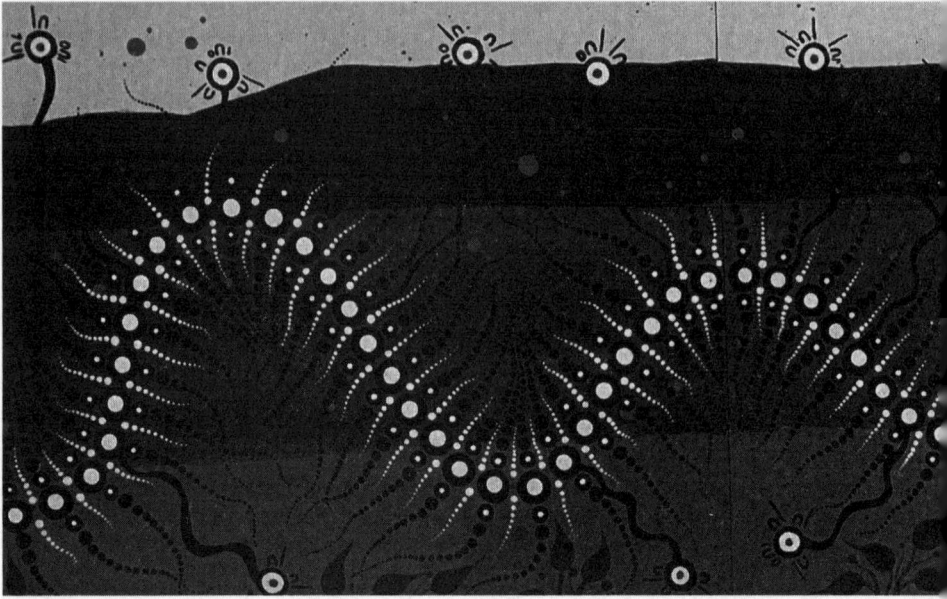

Detail of the Gurawul painting (Image reproduced with permission from Yuin Gurandji senior men)

We have many keen visitors coming to the farm to learn about our methods, but on this particular day we had an Aboriginal university student, Cal Callope, who came to talk about her food sovereignty thesis. We weren't to know that Cal would soon work for Black Duck as Projects Manager.

The farm is always busy. We were helping a few young men in difficulty or distress to talk through their problems and just relax on the farm. These are the sons of old mates who find the life of an Aboriginal person to be full of struggle.

I was glad to get to bed, but restless with the pain of having to insist on the Aboriginal right to run our business our way. The pain of the young men sleeping on the farm was also a weight. I watched the stars in their slow wheel and hoped.

I took the car to Bega to get serviced the next morning and it was a relief to get away. I had coffee next to Candelo Books in

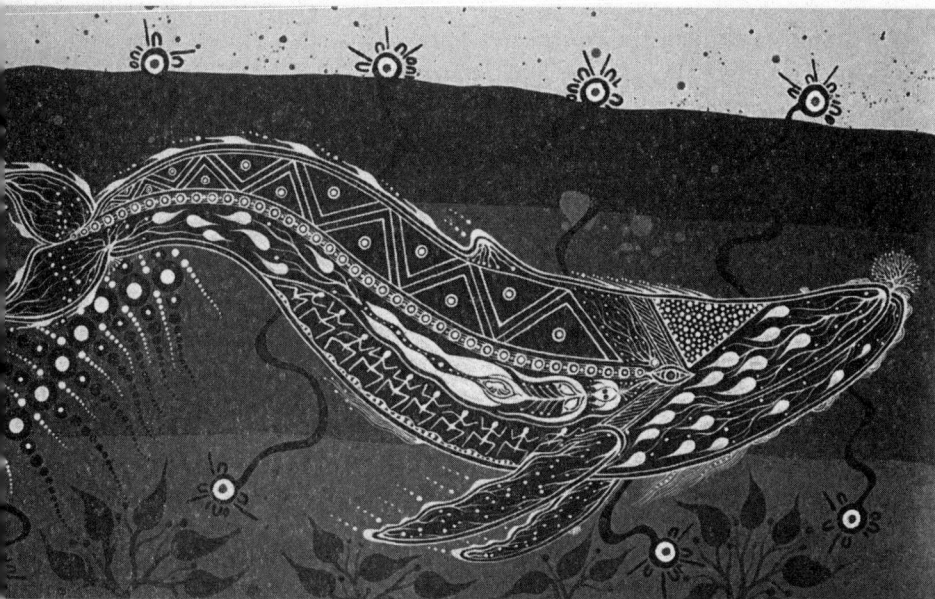

the main street – that bookshop is always a delight. Wangarabell attracted many compliments as she sprawled on the footpath. The break allowed me to relax so I went over to Maggie and Rosie's Antiques and bought two cabinets, which had once belonged to a huge old wardrobe or something. They looked a bit divorced from their purpose, but I bought six glass spheres to cover the screw holes that had once joined the little cabinets to the main piece. I'm really happy with the way they look glued into position.

The possum skin cloak my family made me for my seventieth birthday is draped across them and so it feels like my bedroom is finished. It's a real sanctuary for me. All those diverse bits of recovered wooden furniture following their individual lore and providing comfort.

I had to get up early to cut limbs off a cherry tree and some stringybarks so that Mick from Cann River could work on the roads with his truck and bobcat.

As the day warmed, the horses got harassed by the March Flies but Jitti Jitti (Willy Wagtail) flies from horse to horse snatching the flies. It's a lovely relationship between horse and bird.

I saw a Mudlark attending to the tail of a Buru (kangaroo) the other day but the roo seemed to resent it. Is the beak of the Mudlark too sharp? The personalities and habits of all the animals are incredibly compelling and make the land vibrant with story.

Googar

There's an old dead tree in the middle of the yard and most people reckon it should come down, but a hundred birds a day roost on its branches at various times to take advantage of the 360-degree view of the country. A few years ago a Masked Owl was living in one of the several holes and frightened the life out of my neighbour from across the river, Tony Brindley.

After George Johnson died, Tony looked after his little dog, Mate. Tony came over to clean up some weeds on George's place and the owl screamed at him. The scream of a Masked Owl has made tougher men than Tony start dripping.

Anyway, no, I won't be cutting down the tree. Sunday 13 February, Lyn and I saw a little Googar (goanna) sidle down the trunk and make its way across the paddock toward the house. But no self-respecting Birran Durran Durran was going to stand for that, so they shrieked at, bombed and stalked the creature until it disappeared.

I knew it would be somewhere close and suspected he was hunting duck eggs but old Wangarabell found him in the compost bin. He'd been sliding around in the moisture and shone like a jewelled prince. The black and yellow stripes and stars are fitting for the royalty they believe they hold.

We sent him on his way from the bin where he'd been hunting rats. I was happy about that but Wangarabell wasn't so, goodbye Googar.

We picked more plums and stewed them. I love stewed fruit on cereal in the morning and it doesn't hurt in a curry either.

I needed to take Lyn back to Gipsy to put her chooks to bed and on the way back we met Dale and Carla (yeah, I taught them both) who had been picking apples on their property just upstream from Yumburra. They passed across a bag as our boats idled in the stream. Beautiful day.

I was busy the next day with management issues and some writing jobs. I finished a foreword for David and Rebecca's new Warndu book titled *First Nations Food Companion Cookbook*, and added another verse to the 'Three Rivers' song I began with Uncle Max, and it was a relief to swim in the warm water of the river. Later I caught two lovely bream while juggling phone calls about the sad business of having to stick up for our culture against people who pretend to love us.

I went to Pambula to talk to Todd and Ruth of Wild Rye's Bakery about grain and flour products and the upcoming EAT Festival. They are really lovely people and have helped us a lot without having asked for a thing in return. They allow us to use a container behind the bakery where our fellas are threshing and drying grain. The aroma is truly sensational.

Australia will come to love Australian grain. But how will they ensure that Aboriginal people are part of the industry? That question again, but sometimes you need to repeat something a hundred times before a bell rings in the colony.

Mick was still plugging away on the roads and I went and picked up four large pipes to act as culverts to take water away from the road.

When the pipes were set into the road below the dam, we got ready to drive to Apollo Bay to see Jack and Shelly and granddaughter Lily, and of course, Clark, the world's gentlest dog.

It's ten hours to the Bay so we camped at the infamous Kansas City Motel in Bairnsdale and had a really lovely meal at the Terminus Hotel. Bell sleeps in the car, tolerates the motel and never complains about the length of the journey. She is a joy.

Lyn and I drove on to Apollo Bay, but a stone thrown by a mower smashed Lyn's passenger side window. That slowed us down but we had a great night with Jack and Shell and Lily, who has her own very definite personality. She is a watchful kid, so, if you say something she looks at you to work out who you are.

Took the peaceful Clark for a walk on Jack's track. I heard a little bird I'd heard before at Cape Otway. It is a very loud and insistent call, birrita birrita driit driit. I searched for it but couldn't find it. I'm sure it's a scrubwren or thornbill but nothing on the bird app matches it. Really intriguing. Clark was no help. (I tracked the bird down at Gipsy Point in autumn 2023 and, with the help of Lyn and the bird app, identified it as the beautiful Rose Robin.)

Got back to the farm on Saturday 19 and met up with the Kempsey mob and Aunty Dolly. We had a long yarn. Aunt is a real comic. But a thoughtful one. Her humour belies the seriousness of her commitment to Aboriginal culture.

The Kempsey mob are interested in the foods we are growing and so we sat around the campfire to talk about growing our foods and ensuring Aboriginal employment in the industry.

Gurandgi Robert, Amiey and family arrived just to have a yarn. It was lovely of them to drive all the way. Robert works hard for Gurandgi lore and comes to every event. It was reassuring to host them on the farm as all the disturbance and pain washing around is unsettling. Sitting down and talking culture without having to explain the entire history of Australia is a relief.

I was on the tractor trying to finish off the road surfacing but the Kinchela Boys Home people came to have a yarn and then the Maritime Union people Joe, Evan and Shalah. All lovely people, but the day disappears pretty quickly.

I sought the refuge of the river and caught a lovely bream to give to Pat Wilkinson, Lyn's Gipsy neighbour and great friend. Pat is a highly intelligent ex-doctor and a great friend to Aboriginal people. She worked for a long time with Uncle Jim, a staunch advocate for his people. Jim and Pat worked closely in Aboriginal health for decades. Unfortunately, Pat died early in January 2023 aged ninety-four.

Lyn and I took the boat out on the lake just to get away from the phone and drifted about just having a drink and talking about kids and jobs and fish. Lyn described it as a small oasis of peace, every bird softly winding up the day's activity, the world becoming quieter and quieter, stiller and stiller as the sky finds its last colour.

When we separated all those years ago we had stopped finding that time to talk at dusk. The river is so calm and stolid that it forbids hectic conversation. Talk flows at the speed of an idling bream dreaming by the rocks.

Next morning there was mist hanging low over the river, unusual for this time of year, but it made for a quiet and masked journey. The farm, however, was in full swing with Nathan doing great work in the gardens.

That night I watched the ABC episodes of *People's Republic of Mallacoota* and was shocked that it was so negative. The whole six weeks was a nightmare but to listen to grievances against the authorities sounded cheap and churlish. The plan, instituted by one of our coppers and the local head of Parks, was formulated a decade

Nathan weeding the Murnong garden bed

earlier but its structure meant that the town's readiness was probably responsible for the fact that no lives were lost in the town apart
from Freddy Becker who died of a heart attack while fighting the fire
at Maramingo.

Individuals and ad hoc teams were also wonderful, so to hear
people carping and finger-pointing was upsetting. We've got all these
rights these days but little responsibility. I can't think of a time where
debate has been less gracious and respectful.

Meanwhile, work continued unabated with manager issues press-
ing and getting ready for the ABC to arrive for filming. The show
is called *Movin' to the Country*, but I still haven't seen it. Grace is
also filming and Malyan Winsor arrived and I showed him around
the farm and introduced him to the crew. His mum, Sharon, is the
dynamo behind Indigiearth food company. I felt mean that I had so
little time to spend with the young man.

I had a late Zoom talking to earnest young food sustainability
people and I was flagging in front of the screen. Since Covid I have
been averaging one of these online sessions a day and they take so
much energy, but while I was talking, I saw six to eight White Kites
circling above the Water Ribbon and Cumbungi dams.

The Black-shouldered Kites and Nankeen Kestrels are never seen
in numbers greater than two and here was a flock. It made me wonder
if they were Letter-winged Kites. I haven't seen any in the district
since the seventies. I was trapped by the screen and couldn't leave
to investigate. When I finished the Zoom they were gone, but their
beauty and wildness had lifted my spirit.

I filmed with Grace the next day then jumped on the tractor to
smooth some sections of the road because rain was on the way. Some
more food nerds rocked up and I had a cup of tea with them and tried
not to look at the tractor parked on the hill. For a man trying to be
a hermit I'm failing badly. I like people but not so many at once.

Noel and Trish arrived later so we could organise Black Duck Foods after the departure of the manager. We had a great meeting but much better yarns. Noel is a vivid raconteur and it distracted me from the problems of the farm … and my inability to achieve hermithood.

The rain came and I had to clear drains and shore up culverts and pipes. I've been doing it all my life and controlling water flow is restful work, like playing as a child, except the pick and shovel are heavy and the back is no longer supple.

On Sunday 27 we spent all day on the lake with Noel and Trish. We had breakfast at Amy's tiny cafe in Mallacoota after a glorious boat trip. Amy is the daughter of my cricket captain, Presto, but she has survived that impediment quite well. Presto is an Energizer Bunny and works and plays nonstop. Amy has inherited that work ethic; and the smile.

We picked up mussels in the lake, both Bimbla (Blood Mussel) and Dalgal (Black Mussel) but had no luck with the fish. I was hoping to get the boat ready for Noel and Trish to take out overnight where their fantasy of cooking fresh prawns, fish and mussels on a beach somewhere on the lakes had them sighing in their beer. I'm sure their recovery from the fire that took their house is not complete. May never be.

Last day of February was taken up by SBS filming and a Zoom with Melbourne University's Dookie campus. That night Noel, Cooma, Nathan and I went up to Merimbula for the premiere of Cooma's film on the damage being done by brumbies in the Alpine National Park. Richard 'Cooma' Swain has been fighting valiantly to save the mountain wetlands.

Uncle Ozzie Cruse was there too and grabbed my arm as we were leaving and had an urgent conversation about the community. He's really worried, the old man, worried not just about the state of things but the slippage of sand through the narrow funnel of his time.

I owe a lot to Uncle Oz because he was one of the many elders who stuck up for me when the right-wing press were trying to destroy me. One day he stopped me in the street at Eden and shook his finger at me, 'Don't you ever, ever, stop what you are doing.' It was so comforting to have his support.

Rain and Rivers

It was 1 March and the currawongs, wattlebirds, bowerbirds, magpies and galahs were all raucous in the uncovered apple tree near the woodshed. The apples must be just ripe enough for them to puncture the skin.

Satin Bowerbird and our dog's bowl

I am covering for the Black Duck general manager for the next few weeks and this, combined with farm work, is a challenge. The rain is also complicating things. Nathan and his brother Mook had to go home early as the news came through that the Towamba River was rising. They've been getting more rain than us. Turns out they were too late and had to go on to Eden.

The Towamba is a great river. I used to catch beautiful bass under the bridge before clear felling forestry caused tons of sand to choke up the bass holes. I once saw a mulloway chase a school of fish into the shallows near the mouth. When the fish realised they were trapped there was an eruption of fish flipping and spinning in the air. It was a remarkable sight.

More rain was coming our way, so I was on the tractor trying to shore up the new road work so that we didn't lose all the expensive gravel.

It was still warm so I had a swim in the river and a little way downstream four swans were sailing with typically serene elegance. I must have unsettled the two adults because they took to the air.

I was speculating whether the two smaller ones were this year's hatchlings in their adult plumage, when a Mirridar (Sea Eagle) flew out of a tree and attacked one of adults.

The eagle wheeled about and was homing in on the swan that had been knocked out of the air when the eagle saw me and banked away. The habit of swans and many other birds to distract predators from their flightless young has its own hazards; sniping eagles being one of them.

I once saw a young fledgling attacked while in a family group. It disappeared under the water and I thought it must have been killed, but thirty seconds later it bobbed up and swam into a patch of protective Phragmite Reeds. How did it keep under for so long? What lessons are young birds taught when no one is watching?

Early one morning down near the Bandstand on the Jinoor I was fishing in pearly dawn light. I had two lovely fish in the keeper bag so I wasn't trying too hard, just enjoying the rising sun. The Bandstand is a funny name for a sand bar but one old local has another map which suggests it used to be labelled Sandbank. Cartographer's clerical error?

Anyway, just as I was thinking of pulling in my lines, I saw a young Mirridar gliding along the bank with its talons stretched out in the striking pose.

It plunged its feet into the water and latched on to a huge mullet but when it tried to take off the fish was too heavy for the young bird to lift. It was a case of the monkey reaching into the jar to grab the banana, not being able to withdraw its hand but unwilling to let go of the prize.

The young Mirridar was in that predicament and as it mulled the conundrum its feathers began to get heavy with water. What to do? Well, it rested for a moment and then swept its wings forward in a rowing motion and rowed the fish to shore and dragged it up onto the beach. I don't expect to see that even repeated but very glad I was up early to see it.

I'd been picking nectarines and tomatoes as quick as I could and converting them into sauces and pickles. I got the crop in and did a bit of weeding and when I looked up to straighten my back I saw a whole mob of swifts plummeting like warheads across the paddocks. Storm coming. I battened down the hatches and was bringing in garden tools ahead of the rain when the swifts hurtled across the paddock at knee height and I couldn't move.

There were a hundred or more and it felt like an attack but, for the swifts, I was just one more obstruction. Years earlier I was leading a tour of the Cape Otway Lighthouse and when I swung open the heavy door onto the balcony, swifts were bulleting toward us and veering away at the last minute.

I had Irish and Asian tourists and they were mesmerised. Lyn did a tour later and the same thing was happening. I think they were using the white bulk of the tower to highlight insects or maybe using the obstacle as an entrapment for their prey. Anyway, the tourists got their money's worth.

I used to like the overseas tourists because most understood what a war looked like and many knew what a genocide looked like so they understood my story of Australia's history straight away.

Young German tourists were very interesting. They were hyperconscious of their country's human rights record but determined never again to be part of anything like the Holocaust. They understood the Invasion of Australia in a visceral way.

Many Australian men, on the other hand, wanted to argue whether any Aboriginal people were killed and when confronted by incidents and numbers would often conclude, 'Well, they weren't using the place anyway.' My feeling is that Australia is about to leave that opinion behind, but perhaps I show too much faith.

Aboriginal people manipulated trees to produce significant shapes. Some were for intricate cultural purposes and others were simple directions.

Autumn

Heron

*Every autumn I wait for the rains to begin, reviving paddocks,
filling dams and creeks, soaking the gardens. There are always
floods, or too much water in an inconvenient place, our
responsibility is to watch the land, learn the drainage pattern
and adapt to it. Any problems after that belong to you.*

Nothing Like a Good Flood

The rain was getting heavier and I was nervous about the roads. There's a sense of helplessness once you've opened all the drains and culverts as best you can. You can only listen to rain hammering on the roof, watch the swamp expand and river rise, and hope.

Lyn went to a Glossy Black-Cockatoo ID workshop that looked at a block of land at Gipsy Point where the frequent cool burning by the owner had allowed many Casuarina plants to survive the fires and leave a haven for these magnificent old friends.

Graham Berry owns that land and has always taken an interest in Aboriginal history, and for a decade has been trialling cool burn techniques. He's a cantankerous old curmudgeon but he arrived like that in 1975 when we recruited him straight from Teachers' College. He loved the place and never left.

He was a science teacher and taught kids about gravity by throwing eggs off the school roof. Now he is trying to protect the habitat of a seriously endangered bird.

There are still numbers of these rare and beautiful birds but how they escaped the fires is a mystery. Lyrebirds and reptiles will shelter in wombat burrows but how other birds and mammals survive is not well known. After fires I saw lyrebirds and kangaroos immediately after the fire had passed. Where had they been? I see very little evidence of dead animals after fires but we know the losses must have been huge. Anyway, the survivors were greeted with enormous joy and relief.

The rain kept falling and the river had a roiling motion, dangerous. I shifted *Nadgee* further up into Yumburra Creek and put her on a long line fore and aft, because in the last flood she ended up on top of the jetty and when the flood receded I could barely move her.

Lyrebirds somehow managed to stay safe during the fire

While I was working to shift the boat there were hundreds of birds feeding noisily. One White-browed Treecreeper was frantically trying to prise a piece of bark off a Melaleuca. We all love a decent flood.

The rain was heavy overnight and I was working hard to save the road. I had to do a plants workshop with Twofold Aboriginal Corporation in preparation for the new camp park we are building at Jigamy. I got across the water cascading out of the Water Ribbon Dam but worried about getting back.

The water was up to the wheel hubs when I did get back which made me worried about getting off the property to go to Adelaide Writers' Week.

I decided to open up the hill track the next morning so I could catch the plane. It was still raining and I feared for the road.

I love the Adelaide festival but on one panel I had a gent who was damning with faint praise. One right-wing commentator blew a riot whistle and people went to water as if the people who hate Aboriginal people actually know what they're talking about. Screaming, shouting and outrage suffices in the place of information.

Fortunately, most people go back to the original reports I referred to in *Dark Emu* and *Convincing Ground* and can see how differently they speak about the country and what we were taught in school. But I find it very bruising and disappointing that some in academia are so reluctant to let go of the myth of a bloodless invasion.

Bunjil got back into the duck pen while I was away. And that was a very bloody invasion. Mick came up to the farm to check the road and found the eagle in the yard. He trapped the bird in his jacket and then took a video of himself unwrapping the indignant eagle and releasing it like a fairground magician.

Sir Francis Drake was badly injured so Lyn and our neighbour, Kate, moved all the ducks to her place and put Sir Francis in the apple orchard and gave him a good spray of antiseptic, but he was not looking good.

Meanwhile, I talked about native grains at a workshop and then flew from Adelaide to Canberra and met up with Lyn and we drove on toward Sydney for the second of Unc's ceremonies.

As we drove toward Wollongong we had to dodge around closed roads and eventually got to the escarpment, awed by the giant cliff faces where brand new waterfalls were springing up everywhere. The rain continued to be heavy and persistent so I was feeling bleak about Sir Francis and the road.

On Saturday 12 March we attended Uncle Max's service. I was surprised to find it was in Scott Morrison's evangelical church, but the Gurandgi gathered outside in the gardens and reflected on the old man's influence on us.

The memorial went for over seven hours and the tension between sections of family overflowed. It was very upsetting.

Gurandgi prepare fire outside the church

After the memorial I had to fly back to Adelaide for the rest of the festival. While I was away Sir Francis died leaving Lyn feeling wretched. I felt pretty wretched too but I had to do a Zoom to receive the Australian Humanist of the Year award, do some media interviews for WOMADelaide and, finally, a panel with Charlie Massy.

I met up with old friends Helen and David at the festival and was overwhelmed by the numbers of Blackfellas coming up to share stories. It lifted my spirits to see their hope and enthusiasm.

Eventually I was able to leave and fly to Canberra and drive home to the farm, grateful that I was able to dodge around all the closed roads.

It is encouraging to do the Zooms and panel shows for sustainable farming and Aboriginal inclusion. I did three today, including one on soil carbon. It is impossible to say no to such worthy causes. Then I had to drive to Melbourne for an event to support the book I wrote with Vicky Shukuroglou, *Loving Country*.

Democracy's Slow Wheel

Lyn spent the next few days battling the bureaucracies to begin a mulching program around the perimeter of Mallacoota as a fire prevention measure. The politics is wilting but she has been trying to get this program established since before the big fires. Some blokes want to scorch and bulldoze all the bush and some can't bear the thought of even the smallest flame, even though many of our orchids depend on fire.

Thelymitra: *Sun Orchids were prolific after the fire*

This is the information battle required for a nation to learn how to deal with the country they took by force but without respect for the knowledge accumulated over 100,000 years. When that conversation starts, so can the healing of Country and citizens.

While in Melbourne I did another Zoom and then events at the Blak & Bright First Nations Literary Festival at the State Library of Victoria, followed by AgriFutures, Indigenous Knowledge Institute, First Languages Australia and a session with Paul Gordon, an Aboriginal writer and cultural leader.

I really enjoyed talking with Paul, but I felt sorry for the young Koori organisers who do all the work and then have to sit through

Monarch Caterpillar

interminable meetings with their faculties. I miss out on most of that side of the work now and I'm not sorry.

Lyn wrote that while fighting the good fight for sensible fire control the difficulty of the tightrope was daunting but she was uplifted when she saw 'bushes covered in Monarch Caterpillars and their dainty little gold braceleted cocoons. A butterfly emerged, crumpled wings like folded velvet.' It is those moments of joy and wonder that make tedious work bearable.

On Saturday 19 I spoke with Leah Hills about her RidgeWalk project, a collection of stories about the Yarra Valley. I began my story and enjoyed the total immersion in words although the foundation of the project makes me nervous; editorial by a committee of earnest people.

In the afternoon I went to the MCG and saw Richmond get beaten and then had to walk back to Carlton. It felt like a long way.

I went to Blak & Bright to support other writers including Aunty Barb Nicholson and Aunty Evie. These are old mates whose relentless pursuit of justice for Aboriginal people has inspired me for decades.

I finished the RidgeWalk story and then had a long Zoom with Gurandgi as we tried to tread lightly between the divisions in Uncle's family.

The next day I met with Melbourne University staff in the Agriculture faculty and spoke with all the Koori students. We began building a strategy to publish Beth Gott's unpublished papers and I enjoyed honouring the Aboriginal botany work of that old warrior. Beth's work on Murnong was one of the foundations for *Dark Emu*.

I had to do a Zoom with the University of Massachusetts on decolonising museums but then had the pleasure of walking through Zena Cumpston's Emu Sky exhibition, where I was moved to see Badger Bates's digging sticks and Jonathan Jones's wooden shovels. I think the shovels, which pre-date the invasion, should really alert

Australia to our shared humanity. The human brain coming up with the same object to solve the same problem on different continents.

I'd like to see the shovels and the stone hoes used as a unifying lesson for all Australian students. Forget the huff and puff of those insistent on Western superiority and focus on the shared humanity.

The Wood Grub Philosophy

Above the entrance to the exhibition I was struck by a panel of Aunty Joy Wandin's painting of Red Gum Grub tunnels beneath bark. I stopped abruptly because it was such a vivid reminder of something I tried to paint myself. I wanted to honour an insect etching on a log that caught my eye while doing a banal interview with someone sent out to do a magazine piece on the farm.

I was stupefied with boredom and turned to the forest as a way of surviving the hour when the pattern captured me. I have drawn, painted and dreamt that etching many times.

I had spoken to Uncle Max about my fascination with these grub etchings and he just smiled and drew one in the dust of the road where we were standing at the time discussing the river divisions at Nimmitabel. He tapped at his drawing until he saw the realisation dawn on me. Grubs drawing rivers on trees.

Aunty Joy's image was accompanied by the information that Wurundjeri means the grub that etches the red gum. It encouraged me to think of the Yumburra scrawl and Uncle Max's Nimmitabel drawing as symbols for the farm.

I am so warmed by the Old People's philosophy. The Old People took as their supreme beings such humble creatures: Wurundjeri, the Wood Grubs; Ganai, Blue Wren; Yuin, Black Duck; Dharug, Murnong tuber. This identification with the small, the modest, holds such promise for a world which takes as its symbols the fierce and the deadly; tigers, snakes, lions, bombers, sharks. Looking close, looking small, reveals a very different way of approaching the world.

I had to do another couple of Zooms and then I finished the RidgeWalk essay and emailed it to Leah but the images of the runes created by blind insects twined and netted in my dreams.

I had breakfast the next day with Marcia Langton and Barry Judd from Melbourne University to talk about holding a seminar about preserving Aboriginal intellectual property in the agricultural sector. It numbs me to think of the difficulty of bringing this about.

I flew to Sydney to receive the Australian Society of Author's Medal for services to literature. I had a long yarn with Donna Ingram, who did the Welcome to Country, and it calmed me. We then listened to Nyadol Nyuon, the sister of Richmond footballer Bigoa Nyuon, speak about her family's struggle. I'm not trying to be gratuitous by including Bigoa in a comment about his sister, the lawyer and human rights activist, it is to emphasise what Australia has gained by providing havens for refugees.

Nyadol is a champion, a victor over incredible hardship. Donna and I glanced at each other ruefully. Not because we were cynical, far from it, we were moved by the speech, but Australians often opine about the failure of Aboriginal people to do the same and then look at us sternly. The magnitude of the injury acquired when losing the entire continent and then having your history denied has to be better understood. How could a human brain and heart cope with such total loss? Not just life and limb, but to lose the land your people had ordered you to look after as if it were your mother. And on your watch it was lost! The trauma still reverberates, but we Aboriginal people must resist the place of shame the colony has designated for us. Know your history, practice the culture, resist, live!

And to mark that clarion call I heard that brother Gurandgi Shuluman had just been given a baby girl and that five other Gurandgi are expecting children.

On the Thursday I flew from Sydney to Melbourne and picked up my car. I can't remember how I had organised for it to be there but it marks the craziness of this schedule.

I drove on to Orbost and did some more filming for ABC's *Movin' to the Country* with Gabby and Chris from Sailors Grave Brewing. As I have explained, they make the beer, Dark Emu, for which we supply the grain. We get a little percentage from the proceeds and it all goes to Aboriginal students who need a little help. Part of the money goes to the GO Foundation created by Adam Goodes and Michael O'Loughlin, both heroes of mine. I took delight in showing my kids that I had Adam's number in my contacts list.

Adam Goodes was pilloried by football crowds for daring to assert his pride in being Aboriginal. Some critics tried to say that the booing was not because of his skin but because of how he played the game. Had they forgotten he won a grand final for the Sydney Swans while playing on a broken leg? Come on Australia, no more excuses.

One of the students we support has just joined the Swans Academy. We are so proud of her. She's also a great artist and writer and has won gold medals for rowing. And she dances her traditional dances. Look out!

I finished the filming and drove the extra couple of hours to the farm. There I was greeted by six new ducklings, like Shuluman's daughter, life insists on living.

Friday 25 I did some more filming for *Movin' to the Country* and then did another couple of Zooms on sustainability and Aboriginal employment. Afterwards I took the boat down to Gipsy Point to have a Friday night drink with the town. It was relaxing but I bailed out early to get some sleep.

New life

I named the most colourful duckling Darken after the dog Lyn's Uncle Bob used to have, another lesser marked duckling has become Dusk and the other, uniform yellow ducklings will have to wait for names until the grandkids are consulted.

I wasn't picked in Mallacoota's grand final cricket side! What, Presto, you can't find a place for a seventy-four-year-old of limited agility whose bowling arm no longer rotates and hasn't been able to hit the ball off the square for twenty years? It turned out to be a great game anyway. Mallacoota occasionally join forces with Eden to create one team for B grade and this was the case for 2022. It was an incredible celebration as all three Eden grades won their respective grand finals. How many clubs have been able to say that?

I was happy, of course, but it's not the same if you don't play and no one can tell you it is. I had my car so I went home early, leaving mayhem behind me. None of those cricketers are likely to see such a result again. It is so hard to do but if anyone is going to do it it is Eden with help from Mallacoota. Both clubs are well run and I have enjoyed two decades of playing in their company. But I'm sad that I'm no longer able to do it. It was a long quiet drive home.

The next day Lyn and I did the Glossy Black-Cockatoo ID count. We didn't find any birds but did see a lot of trees where they had been feeding. Signs of hope. And, in the spirit of hope, I reinforced the duck house roof with stronger wire mesh. Hope for the ducklings.

I worked on Aboriginal food videos for school kids while Chris and Mook worked on adjusting the threshing machine for our smaller grains. Lyn spent the day doing administration for Black Duck. It absorbs a lot of our time but has to be done until we can find someone else to do it.

The preparation for the arrival of the Murrumbidgee Landcare mob is an example of that work. We need to spread the word but we put in a lot of effort for not much return. We have to charge for these services because, while we're doing these educational and research programs, we're not actually doing the regular farm work.

There's no doubt that it produces rewards for us but they are not monetary. We met the participants at our gate on 31 March and performed a smoking ceremony despite drizzling rain.

We learnt a lot about the catering side of things and thanks to Noel and Trish, did it ourselves, making bread from our grains and cooking our tubers. Everyone was really impressed by the flavours and we were relieved to see how enthusiastically our food was relished.

On April Fool's Day we took the guests on a forest walk and gardens tour. Chris and Nathan were superb in how they explained the story of the farm and our plans for empowering local community.

Bread cooked in the fire pit for our guests

The morning tea featured our Kangaroo Grass flour Johnny Cakes and they were swooped on by the guests who couldn't stop talking about them for the rest of the day.

I stayed at Lyn's house with Noel and Trish and we had breakfast in town at Amy's cafe. She's a joy that kid. I'll never forget how she taught me what shots are one long cricket afternoon at our end of season trip. I was complaining to her that, when washing up, there were small glasses inside bigger glasses. She explained the theory of spirit shots. I was astounded. I've never been interested in spirits so I really couldn't see the point. But her father is a fan, a big fan.

The rain got really heavy so I had to race back to the farm and check that the road culverts were running properly. While I was there I continued the work of cladding a new, more weatherproof, duck house. The girls were nervously fascinated by my interference in their abode.

Rain and Pigeons

April 3 and still raining. My confidence in the roads holding up was fading. *Nadgee* was still coping but the ground was saturated and you could see runnels of water everywhere. It continued to rain up at Bombala so the rivers would begin to rise and slow the water coming off the land, backing it up into the swamps and dams.

Visitors came to the farm and I found myself having to defend the Wave Hill Walk-off as a rebellion against slavery not an attack on the fabled Australian grazing industry, Sid Kidman and R.M. Williams, the Akubra and the Driza-Bone, the uniform of the iconic Australian cattleman.

Kidman is lauded for drought proofing his herds by taking up more and more land so he could move cattle around the country to wherever there was grass.

But on whose land and at what expense were those cattle moving across the landscape? It was a dismal argument and I made little progress against Australia's assumption of its glory and mastery of a savage land. My argument is that if those leases couldn't survive without slave labour, the lease should have been revoked.

Afterwards, I sat on the deck watching the rain and feeling the difficulty of having a reasoned argument in this country. It's about identity but Australia often shuts off an investigation of fact by an adherence to myth.

Why do some Australians feel so affronted by pale-skinned Aboriginal people? We are their children, our mothers gave birth to their heritage. There is an intelligent discussion to be had here but the press often seems to prefer the heat of conflict, rather than the cool of reason.

While mired in this bleak prospect a White-headed Pigeon landed very clumsily on the verandah rail. They are so beautiful but would never get a job with the Bolshoi Ballet. These birds used to be an exceptionally rare visitor but, as a result of global warming and the different vegetation profiles that are establishing, birds like Crimson Honeyeaters, Channel-billed Cuckoos and others are now common visitors and some may be residents.

We are still struggling with the loss of Uncle Max and the competing personalities and claims are wearing everyone down. It's a sad fact of death that the living have so much trouble accepting it.

The Mallacoota fire show series *People's Republic of Mallacoota* is beginning on ABC TV and it makes for uncomfortable viewing but at least I got to see our lovely dogs, even if Bulla is no longer with us. I miss his blockheaded foolishness and constant positivity. He always thought joy was just a walk around the farm away and he would insist that you joined him in his excitement. Miss you, old mate. You could always make me laugh.

It was still raining lightly but with a glimpse of watery sun every now and then. Rosco helped me finish the duck house, which I really appreciated. I find the heavy lifting hard these days. Ross Knight is a Wurundjeri man and also a member of the Gurandgi lore group and a great musician.

Then there was a Black Duck board meeting and afterwards I jumped on the tractor to work on the roads, but all the newly installed pipes had been washed out below the Water Ribbon Dam. The force of the water was so great that one of them was bent clean in half. I jammed it against a tree and straightened it out and it opened up like a resurrected concertina. Didn't look too bad. They are large ribbed plastic pipes and easy to move about with the tractor but replacing the pipes is difficult and requires more gravel.

So much water comes over the road at that point that I think we will have to lower the profile of the road so that we don't create an obstruction to the flow. It is disheartening to see so much work wasted. The crossing is now very rough. Two-wheel drives will have no hope. It was over the ute's door sill the day before.

Mook and I reinstalled the overflow pipe from the dam and secured it by tying wire between two star pickets and then hammering down the posts to fix the pipe tight. Once again, I appreciated the help. The pipes are light enough but after a few hours slopping through water and mud, the funny side of it begins to pale.

The Wallagaraugh is rising slowly and the White-faced Herons are looping around the farm in their elegant courtship.

Last night two disoriented swallows battered my bedroom window and I had to get up and lead them away so they could find their old roost on top of the back door light. People look askance at the pile of guano that is building up there. But if you could see how comfortable they are you'd find it hard to evict them. They are friends and, like the dogs, they cheer me up.

Lyn's road has been washed away but she is more concerned about an old spider, two of whose legs she inadvertently amputated with a fly screen. It has been around for months but since the rain it has been in the house constantly. Lyn's sister-in-law is staying with her and she is a fervent cleaner and Lyn is worried the spider will get vacuumed.

Next morning the whole world was shrouded in a dense mist so it became a day for little jobs: final fix on duck house roof, weeding Munyang and Murnong gardens, tying up plants blown over by the wind, harvesting fruit.

While making a frugal dinner I fielded a lot of calls from Gurandgi who are doing their best to ensure Uncle is sent off with respect. I had to go down to fix the bilge pump on *Nadgee* and take her back to her jetty which it was now surfacing after the retreat of the river. I'm always amazed at how the rough old jetty copes with the volume of water going by. She is sheltered from the main current but even so, sticks and branches threaten to build up against her flank.

The jetty has a bit of give so she shudders a little as the water rises and I think that little movement helps shake off some of the flotsam coming downstream. She is always amazingly free of debris. She looks a fright but she lasts.

The Jacky Winters are back around the house after having spent summer around the Grey Box trees at the buna, the old dance ground. They are such good company. They talk constantly and vary their conversation from season to season. The twitch of their white-banded tail is an animated part of the day, eye-catching and encouraging.

Some visitors curious about the farm got blocked by a fallen tree so I had to go and rescue them. While I was doing that I came across neighbours Chris Parker and Patch Brackley musing thoughtfully on escaped cattle. Fences down everywhere. Bit of rain, bit of wind and trees fall regularly. Everyone is busy in a flood.

Inspired by Aunty Joy Wandin's painting at Zena Cumpston's exhibition, I painted Wurundjeri on an old bedsheet so I could use it as a Zoom backdrop when the light is too bright in my office.

The butcherbird called the whole time. This is one of their most vocal seasons. It has an incredible song so while I was painting I listened to the most amazing Australian flute solo.

When Mark, one of our farm crew, comes to work he can impersonate the bird in uncanny fashion. One of the Gurandgi, Alistair Brown, amuses himself at lore camps by doing one bird after another and at times it is hard to pick the real ones from Alistair. It is an old-fashioned habit probably learnt from an uncle or grandfather.

Lyn had to do some interviews for another film on the bushfires and, of course, they wanted to film outside the fire shed in Mallacoota. Some members grizzled. The brigade is sometimes negative and, in the past, has shown almost no interest in the years of work Lyn has put into engaging the town and government agencies in a program to make the town safer. It's like herding blowflies into a lemonade bottle and I don't know how she has the patience. One day someone in the CFA will realise that this was the project that brought the town to actively counteract fire without recreating Dresden.

Chris Parker called in. He is one of my old students from the seventies. Chris has just bought Walker's old house upstream from me. We talked floods, fires and Aboriginal heritage. He's a good bloke, Chris, and one of the few not to curl his lip when the word Aborigine appears in a sentence.

We watched the swallows coursing over the grass in the front of the house. They almost stall as they hover. They must be feeding on hatchings of insects but I don't know which ones. I saw a Jitti Jitti catch a brown and gold butterfly a few days ago and as Chris and I watched we saw the bird catch two more.

Chris remembers the camps we took our students on as the best days of their lives. We thought they were pretty good too. We must have been a sight for the town, us mad hippies leading kids away from the school room and down to the beaches.

We ran a bird elective and often took kayaks out on to the lake to count shore birds. We saw a really unusual bird one year and Steve Wadsworth, an old mate and photographer, got a very grainy photo. The school was a member of the Bird Observers Club but when we posted the photo to them they wouldn't believe us.

We thought it was probably a Beach Stone-curlew but the BOC couldn't be convinced. They sent down an earnest party of twitchers who took their sensible shoes and binoculars all up and down the coast and lakes and came back scarlet of cheek and green of chagrin not having seen hide nor feather of the mythic bird.

They were about to call wrath down upon our heads until one of their wives who had been reading a book while sunbaking on the beach and eating Tim Tams came back with a photo. The curlew had strolled past her feet. Our school was famous for a year in bird circles because, before that, the bird hadn't been seen further south than Newcastle.

Our fame was cemented when another student photographed a Cape Barren Goose striding around the shallows of Devlin's Inlet. Some of our kids were so wild they came to school with straw in their hair and surf wax on their chins. Locking them in a school room for too long each day was a cruelty a hippy couldn't contemplate.

The school kept losing principals so frequently that Oscar Wilde would have called it carelessness. Too frequently I was left in charge of the commune. We experimented in education more often than we practised it but we did create a newspaper that fifty years later is still going, the infamous *Mallacoota Mouth*.

The kids researched and wrote the stories and in editorial sessions we'd be standing around with teenagers wondering how to phrase a delicate story. Yes, the child was saved from the savage dog but why was the saviour naked? Constructing those sentences so as not to offend were a constant part of our school day, the best English and social studies lessons you could ever invent.

The kids really grew up quickly. You couldn't do it today because the risks are so great the Education Department wouldn't tolerate the scandal, but in those days we had no policeman, no doctor, no chemist and no real church so we had to officiate the town ourselves. Someone was pinching boat motors. Some large fisherman caused the thief's teeth to become autumnal. Thereafter the culprit was called Onassis after the shipping magnate.

Yes, the *Mouth* reported on that too without referring to autumn or Greek tycoons.

There was a house fire, which aroused some suspicions, but the counsel of the bar was sought and as people sipped beer and the unusual circumstances were considered it was decided that while several events bordered on the criminal it was thought that the ultimate outcome would be equivocal. The town came to the conclusion that it was best just to help rebuild the back of the house and pretend the fire and other activities hadn't occurred. Justice was served with cold beer and delicacy.

The *Mouth*'s editorial committee, average age fifteen-and-a-half, considered the story and decided not to mention it at all. Was it poor journalism or exquisite discretion and solid justice? The kids' sense of fairness was really refined and compassionate. Journalism today often fails that test.

Forest Dusk and Last Chances

Lyn often drives to the farm at dusk and the forest road is so much higher than the paddocks that the full magnificence of the sunset is revealed. One day she recorded that she was struck 'by the late afternoon light of apricot and deep purple bruises that get more intense as I approach the farm, sometimes just enough light to enjoy on the deck upon arrival'.

Soldiering on despite the loss of two of her legs

Lyn's spider is safe but amazingly industrious.

It begins its day in the bathroom and ends the day in the lounge. The passage of the day is just as intense for the currawongs and bowerbirds who feed on the dogs' leftovers at both houses. Because Bell has been away with Lyn for a few days the dog bowl is empty and the birds stand around on deck rails with a sense of uncomprehending injury.

April 8 and the mist is not as profound as recent days but the trees on the hills are spectral in the dawn light. The Grandfather ceremony I do every day causes me to look closely in each direction and give thanks to Grandfather Sun. The discipline forces me to take notice of the world; observation is not a leisure activity but a daily responsibility.

I had to replace the batteries in the wildlife cameras put in place by a PhD candidate. He sent me a thumb drive of the first six months and it turned out to be a video of someone's wedding. Not a wombat in sight.

The fellas harvested food for the Giiyong Festival but Lyn and I headed to Goulburn for a book event twice postponed by Covid and the fires. We had to stay in an ordinary motel because we had poor old Bell with us. The restaurant was a treat. The manager had a tangle of unwashed hair and puffy eyes and her son served the meals but couldn't stop picking his nose. The steak was inedible so we squirrelled some out to Bell who sniffed it once and looked up at us as if we were passing off last year's dead cat. Perhaps we were.

It was very, very sad; as if this was a family on their last chance. Made us bleak to think how that chance might end.

The book festival sessions went well and it was great to meet the local Aboriginal families who showed us about their town. Afterwards we tried to find the famous lagoon so we could give Bell a good walk. We couldn't find it so ended up having our picnic on a dead-end road, but so quiet that we were surrounded by little birds; honeyeaters, thornbills, Silvereyes and all feeding on agricultural weeds. Mesmerising. Then seven Jitti Jitti turned up and all wanted to speak at once. We wondered if that was an ominous sign or one of solidarity.

The festival panel involved a group of writers wrestling with the idea of misappropriation of Aboriginal culture. Those sessions are stressful because I am supposed to have all the answers and take no offence at any of the questions.

We drove home and got back with an hour to spare before I had to join Brian Nankervis's music show on ABC radio. Lyn drove on to Gipsy Point doing a slalom between various groups of kangaroos and wallabies having group therapy in the middle of Gipsy Road.

Brian let me play Woody Allen, Pete Seeger, The Long Johns and Brenda Gifford. In between we yarned about cricket, the farm, children.

When I woke in the morning I had a shower on the deck that looks down toward the dams and swamps, and two young male Buru were boxing each other studiously like two professors having a dispute about a footnote.

There was a big tree across the track so Chris and I cut it up and I shared the wood with Lyn.

There has been a severe blow-up in one of the local Aboriginal families so tomorrow I have to go to court in Bega to offer support. I have a photo of Uncle Max's grandfather, Uncle Muns, sitting in the front of the same courthouse. I wonder why he was there because,

Uncle Muns outside the Bega courthouse

every time I go, the majority of people at the court are Aboriginal and the extent of their crimes is often so minimal as to appear like intimidation of the race. Or guilty of a bad lawyer or no support. We got a good lawyer, a generous listener, and the result was the best that could be hoped for.

Lyn had to attend a Mallacoota and District Recovery Association meeting at Genoa. Her reception was cool because the town is still insulted by the fact that nobody came to help them. Lyn copped the cold shoulder for other people's crimes.

When locals went to access the fire-fighting water tank during the fire it had been locked. The stupidity of that is hard to comprehend but it was not Lyn's fault, she was in the fire station at Mallacoota as it caught alight. I remember driving a tanker into Genoa a day or two after the fire and I couldn't believe the stiff reception we received. We weren't to know we were the first CFA vehicle they had seen.

The townspeople of Genoa saved the town themselves and were feeling let down by the authorities. The firestorm was so horrific and the sense of abandonment so profound they still haven't got over it.

We drove in from fighting fires for forty-eight hours straight and drove up there the first chance the Duty Officer allowed. It was awkward and sad.

I could understand the feeling because one morning, weeks after the first attack, I radioed in for support while I was fighting a fire at a remote house. After I had finished, I drove out to the crossroads and found six CFA trucks waiting around in a paddock. I had to swallow hard.

The CFA rules are clear about what roads large tankers can safely access but my sense of abandonment was similar to that of the people of Genoa.

On one occasion, I brought a supply of diesel to the upper reaches of the Wallagaraugh. I found an old mate hosing down the edge of the fire but as soon as he saw me he started swearing and waving his arms. He'd been at it on his own for days.

'Where's ya bloody truck, ya mongrel, where were you when we needed you?' He was beyond angry, inflamed by the sight of my uniform. I wore it unchanged for weeks. He wouldn't believe I hadn't come by truck so I had to show him my boat and the diesel I had brought him.

There was so much pain and disappointment in the district that friends sometimes swore at friends, patience rubbed raw by extremity. Most of the time however we just worked together in dogged silence because we knew we'd still be filling backpacks and hosing trees at midnight.

One day, at that hour, I stood in the glowing forest and felt absolutely alone. Later I realised I was right, I was the only person left on that part of the river.

So, I could understand the anger and pain but it didn't mean it was any easier to cop the splashback.

That day in Bega court had me thinking of Uncle Muns late into the night. His father had been the only survivor of a massacre but he still ensured his son received the lore and for the rest of Uncle Muns's life he walked between Bega and Bairnsdale trying to support his people. He walked the whole way, perhaps wanting his feet on the ground, like his old ancestors.

Wednesday 13 featured butcherbirds calling and two Buru boys boxing each other down near the Water Ribbon Dam. The young males are practising what will become full-on warfare when they are older. Right now, they cuff each other and try to find the higher ground. They are not kicking each other yet but later they will lean

Cool, patchy burn

back on their tail and use the coiled energy to punch out with a hind foot at the other's belly. A strike there can do a lot of damage but this morning they are still prancing about the stage like Shakespearean actors with plywood swords.

I worked on the roads all morning and my clutch foot is sore but in the afternoon we had to do a cool burn on the flank of the south paddock, so there was a lot more walking. It was a lovely slow burn through four acres and we laughed to see a praying mantis moonwalk in slo-mo away from our fire. It was a perfect example of the process of cool burning. We see dunnarts and antechinus skipping out of the way and plenty of grasshoppers take to their wings but the sight of that sloth-like insect in stately retreat proved to us that this type of fire is good and safe for Country.

The Grandfather ceremony that morning was graced by rays of light radiating toward the house from the top of the east hill and, at this time of year, there were spider webs everywhere. They cling to the netting of the enclosed gardens and the dew transforms them into nets of jewels.

The dew is our safeguard for the burning regime. This is the lore handed down to us by Jinoor Jack. Jack gave the formula of how to burn to the person who massacred his family, such was his determination that Country be looked after. I often think of his state of mind. So determined to care for Country that he'd share the secret with a heathen.

The formula was to light the fires after the prevailing wind has turned to the west and there have been three dews in a row. Light late in the afternoon and let the cool, moist air put it out as the sun begins to dip.

The fellas helped me enclose the grapevine with netting and put a hood on the woodshed to keep it dry. In the arvo we had another cool burn, which was even better than the day before.

Jinoor Jack's plan was for Wangarabell, but that is just down the road so it's perfect for here too. We've been really pleased with the results and the training going into the fellas. Next year we want to bring out busloads from the community so they can experience the pleasure of the work.

I'd like them to hear about Jinoor Jack too. Jack is said to be buried beneath the old bridge at Genoa but as that was burnt down during the fire and replaced with a pedestrian bridge, with all the earthworks that required, I hope he hasn't been disturbed. It is my ambition to memorialise the man who so loved his country that he would ask his enemy to look after her when he was gone.

Autumn in the East

Already 16 April and while the mornings are crisp it became a gloriously warm day. The fellas weren't there so I had the place to myself and I treasured the privacy. I wandered about in a pair of shorts, or worse, cleaning, emailing, cooking, tidying, pulling weeds. I harvested quinces and stewed them into something which I've called Quince Surprise. It's based on a Membrillo (Spanish paste) recipe. I use less sugar and more lemon juice than the recipe calls for, then I add apples and boil it long enough to get the consistency just right. It's nice in a curry and could probably be used as a jam or on a biscuit with prosciutto. There's a lot of it so it had better be good for something.

The air was warm and companionable, these are the days I fell in love with when Uncle Alf and Dad showed me Mallacoota all those years ago. Far East Gippsland. The air is different, there's a distinctive colour to the sky that I've seen nowhere else.

I will never forget that time as a young bloke looking across the sandflats of Mallacoota Entrance to the blue Howe Range.

It changed me, it talked to me so deeply I could feel my intestines crawling with recognition. I was never the same after that hour. I told myself and the country I would come back to stay. Took me five years but I made it.

This evening Pippin was flouncing about, tossing her head, galloping, desperately trying to engage with Lindsay's mare Chrissy, but Chrissy is a bit of a nark, there's Presbyterian in her somewhere. She flattens her ears and steadfastly refuses to look up from her feeding. She hates feckless hippies but I love Pippin's mad spirit, her curiosity and spunk.

In the languorous air I enjoyed a couple of lovely cold Boag's Draught while contemplating horses and sunsets and wheeling herons. I went inside later and made some peculiar meatbally things which I intended to take down by boat to Gipsy Point drinks on the jetty, except the boat wouldn't start and I had to go by car.

While at Gipsy, our neighbour Heather Cowden told me she wanted to sell Pippin. Probably good for the horse if Heather can't care for her feet and coat, but I will miss that mad personality.

All day I mucked around peeling apples and quinces for stewed fruit. I got the boat going and made it down to Gipsy again to meet Jack, Shell, Lily and Marnie, Justin, Marlo, Alia and Charlee who had gathered at Lyn's for the Easter break. After dinner the boat wouldn't start again so I had to go back to the farm with Marnie and Charlee. Very disappointed not to be on the water because moonlight was flooding the valley, silvering every ribbon and bow of water.

Grandmother did a slow and gracious arc over the house and I was conscious of her passage. She disappeared below the western horizon just before dawn and I saw the whole show from my bedroom. It was very moving and I think I was excited by the presence of family. Lily and Shell have never been to the farm before.

Spider Eggs

I don't believe in Easter but I do believe in kids enjoying romance, adventures and chocolate. I created an Easter egg hunt for the kids that went for four kilometres hoping that it would work off the chocolate.

NOTE FOR LILY AND CHARLEE. (BURROW MAIL 2022)

Now that you're out of bed go straight ahead
To the dark green tree
The Yumburra tree
Look under me
And there I'll be.

There's a rocky road
that winds through the trees
follow it to a corner
that's bent like a knee.

And where there's knees there's legs
So have a look here
there's bound to be eggs.

Rabbits bound and so do hounds
So don't forget to check the ground
Follow the road until you get to the gate
Hunt and gather but don't be late.

Coz down at the old phoenix shed
You'll need to look around
Not straight ahead.
Check the old car and the caravan too
But don't take too long
Because we're waiting for you.

Go careful near the dam
But look at the post
There's lovely things there
That kids like the most.

See the blue house on the hill
The home of the dill
Get up there quick
And get ready to pick

On the verandah be careful
Not to rush around fast
There are presents here too
But they're the last.

The bunny from the land of milk and honey.

The kids were right into the egg hunt and were literally dancing along the tracks and through the bush.

After a long breakfast and yarns I went to start the tractors to fix some holes in the road but the battery was flat again. So annoying because I'm worried about Marnie's car on the broken bits of road.

After lunch we lit a section of grassland to match last week's burns. Even with a heavy dew overnight we were able to get it to trickle along and as Grace was here she could film it. Not sure she knew what to expect.

I loved having the kids there to help with the burn. Jack is now the expert so I let him lead the way and I just dawdled about in the soporific smoke. That's why the Old People loved smoke so much, it is so gently calming. Does it rob us of a bit of oxygen? Sure, but when Kangaroo Grass burns the smoke is like a drug.

Then, as usual, down to the river. Shell played with the kids on the stand-up paddle board and she is very patient and funny. Justin plays with the kids on the paddle board too. He holds it while the kids do cartwheels into the river. They also love an invented game where he tells them a story and there is always a different catastrophe but the same result, they're tipped into the water. If you are anywhere on the farm you can always tell when the new catastrophe has been revealed because of the cacophony of shrieks and splashing that follows.

Jack launched *Fluke* and rowed down to Gipsy Point and Marnie accompanied him part of the way on the paddle board. There's something really special about getting to a town, beach or jetty by watercraft.

I bought the board for the grannies to play on a few summers back and, as it was Christmas Eve, felt like I'd been totally ripped off. Just a bit of foam really. Anyway, it has been used constantly and has produced more shrieks and laughter than a circus and Charlee used it to gain confidence with her swimming. This was the first year she could swim from jetty to sandbar.

Much relaxation and many deep conversations have occurred on that sandbar although Birran Durran Durran is always miffed to have her primary resting site occupied by humans.

The paddle board has survived the fires, by a whisker, and several floods. One year I thought I had lost her in a flood but spied a pale shape up against some Melaleuca saplings down near Poor Georges Creek. I had to swim out to her and then clamber aboard and paddle back to the jetty.

As soon as I was on her I realised that it wasn't flood wrack on her but spiders, water striders and beetles. They swarmed all over me in their relief at having a high point on which to escape the flood. It was a long paddle back against the flood and with a thousand relatives investigating me. I thought of an Australian short story by Michael Wilding, 'As Boys to Wanton Flies'.

The journey with arachnids back to the jetty was a little unnerving but not as bad as could be expected. All insects were on their best behaviour. When I got back to dry land I had to remove my shorts and shake them out and wash myself.

During a flood I am totally alone at the farm so I must have been a study of laundry nakedness. Only Golden Whistlers bothered to remark.

During one flood I nearly killed Dale who lives further up the river. I was lying down in my boat trying to fix the bilge pump when I heard Dale's boat come abreast of the jetty. I struggled out from under the stern deck and called a greeting to Dale who nearly jumped out of his boat. Like me he thought he was the only one on the river.

At least I had my shorts on, it wasn't that frightening.

During that particular flood we collected several canoes, kayaks and bits of boat gear. Goodness knows where it comes from because there are only about three farms upstream of us.

I advertised the reclamation of one yellow canoe for a year with no takers. Did it belong to Golom? Anyway, the grannies now see it as part of the farm.

The weather continued to be good so we all went down to Betka River on Monday 18. The Betka is an institution in Mallacoota. Children are conceived there, have their birthdays there, get married there and later have their ashes cast into the stream. Your entire life can be spent by her waters.

A slow stream winds out of the jungles of the upper reaches and approaches the estuary. My old mate Steve Wadsworth, with whom I taught for years, used to call the last bend Little Africa, and it's true, it is a wild paradise. That stretch of river is the only place where I have seen Spangled Drongoes in Mallacoota and so it is vivid in my memory. The banks are scattered with stone artefacts of course because the river bulges with prawns, mussels, fish and stingrays.

The Betka slides out from under the bridge and eddies on a mass of sandbars where most children and dogs in Mallacoota learn to swim or catch a ball. Then it enters the sea. The last 100 metres is used as an elegant water slide to the surf.

I have a friend who uses the estuary that forms the mouth of Wapengo Lake at Bithry Inlet for the same purpose. Apparently, you can float down that river with a glass of wine and not spill a drop where it's not supposed to go. Julie, one of the people closest to me, and wise counsellor in the matter of words, thinks of the Cuttagee Creek, Bermagui, as the place where she has been happiest.

I carried the wild Australian writer Gillian Mears down to the beach at Bithry for her last swim. Even to think of that makes my heart swell. Such a lively woman reduced to a plank by the multiple sclerosis that assailed her. I was crying by the time I got her back to her car. Read Gillian's books, and you will get an idea of just how wild and wise she was, how committed to the protection of the Earth. She's badly missed.

Vicky, one of my closest friends, accompanied me on a journey down the Towamba River which was so interrupted by stingrays, mulloway and the onset of dark that it was never completed. That journey is legendary in my mind for the pure wildness and danger of the experience. It's a mild and beautiful river but if the motor stops on the boat and you have to swim it back upstream amid a shower of skipjack as a giant mulloway chases them ... well, I hope it was a mulloway. Anyway, absolutely vivid and precious in my mind. Vicky is like Aunty Zelda, if there is a fish, bird, animal or insect about it will make itself known and demand her audience. Her films are intense cameos of nature that draw you into the heart of existence.

Aboriginal Food and Family

I have been trying to get people interested in Aboriginal food products for decades and the food industry is keen but sees our food simply as flavours and has failed to imagine how Aboriginal people can be included in the industry. On the other hand, Black Duck Foods is interested in the staple grain and tubers because, not only are they delicious and good for the soil, they speak for Aboriginal sovereignty. They were permanent crops, tilled and cultivated. Sovereign crops.

Granddaughter Charlee and I packed a box of Munyang (Vanilla Lilies) and took them in to a local restaurant. The owner hardly mentioned the lilies but asked me instead what percentage Aboriginal I was. The owner's imperfect English made understanding each other difficult but, even so, I was shattered by the persistence of Australia's incomprehension of Aboriginal Australia.

There is a market for these tubers, especially in Asian cooking, I was thinking of the restaurant's famous dumplings, but the awkwardness prevented me from coming back with another box. And Charlee put so much work into decorating the box too.

A coolamon full of tubers

Australia's unfamiliarity with its national history creates situations like this all the time.

On Tuesday 14 I noticed that a Cattle Egret was escorting Pippin around the paddock. It was the first time I had seen a Cattle Egret on the farm although they are occasional visitors to other farms. Pippin is such a rebellious soul that she probably tossed her head at her escort which may have found safer company in the more supine cows.

The failure of the boat to start was a nuisance so I went up to Eden to buy a marine battery but that didn't do the trick either. We went fishing in Fluke and I caught a lovely bream near Lyrebird Rocks opposite Gipsy Point.

We celebrated Jack's birthday by playing Sleeping Queens. When that card game finished there was a Duck, Duck, Goose game. Adults fall about laughing but the kids are midway between joy and terror. Anyway, the house was a riot.

We are having some teething problems with the installation of solar power to the tiny houses we use for guest accommodation but I had to leave before it was fixed as I had a gig at the Wheeler Centre in Melbourne with Bill Gammage, who wrote *The Biggest Estate on Earth*. It was a great session. Wheeler's always get a crowd so it's never dull.

When I got home I went to work on the boat trailer so I could get *Nadgee* out of the river and repaired in Eden. Flat trailer tyres, burnt-out compressor, failing brake lights and the usual technical issues meant for a very frustrating day.

Back home there was a bit of a Covid scare as Charlee got crook and then I was off-colour. One of the writing mob in Melbourne rang to say she had Covid so I had to get tested but it was all negative.

Lyn and I went to a frog identification workshop in the Genoa Community Hall and got very enthused. To celebrate I cooked a roast meal for the family on the BBQ firepit. Lyn and I then went down to record frogs at the Water Ribbon and Cumbungi dams. We identified Brown Tree Frog and Bibron's Toadlet. The FrogID app is very good and opens up another world of life on the farm.

I had to get up early to film with the Farmer's Footprint crew. We did a small burn for their benefit and it trickled along quietly and effectively. I made dozens of phone calls to the senior group of Gurandgi as we tried to calm and reassure each other that the upheaval since Uncle's death would pass.

Finally, I got *Nadgee* up to Eden for her repairs and slumped down at Sprout's to have breakfast. I met Ty Cruse there who told me a horrifying story of having a heart attack while driving his truck to

Peron's Tree Frog nestled in a rose

Melbourne. Ty is a lovely bloke and Uncle Ozzie's grandson and it was shocking how close he came to the end. It would have been very hard for the Eden community. There is so much death there. Funerals are constant, often for desperate young people. The aim of the farm is to provide an alternative to that desperation.

People are keen for their kids to work out here but so many Blackfellas don't have cars or licences that it is hard organising transport. The work is hard too and some are a bit surprised by that.

Dramas continue with Uncle Max's various funeral preparations but there was a blessing of light rain on dark and, as a balm, I saw two Owlet-nightjars on the track. I can count on my fingers the times I have actually seen one distinctly, so that revelation was a solace and reassurance.

Ceremony for Uncle

I picked up Jack from the airport and drove on to Narooma for Uncle's next ceremony. The house Jack and I stayed in was a bit peculiar but not quite as strange as the Tibetan-type meal we had. We were a little sombre at the prospect of crossing over to Barunguba (Montague Island) in the morning hoping that there would be no outbursts of hurt feelings. It's very delicate.

We gathered at the jetty at dawn but there were no dramas and we sailed to the island on a beautiful Friday morning with about twenty-five Gurandgi. The ceremony was dignified and conducted in silence. It was physically taxing and psychologically nerve-racking, but Cooma, Macca and Dean did a great job. I spent a long part of the ceremony next to Jack. It was just how the pattern worked itself out, but it was hugely comforting and reassuring to have his company.

Later the lads had a swim in the harbour and I was very tempted but I had run my race, emotionally exhausted.

On Saturday we went to the fish traps at Mystery Bay and it was wonderful to hear the young men talking about what they had learnt about this site from Uncle Max, really encouraging, and proof that the lore could continue.

We had a long reflection at Mystery Bay Cottages and people spoke well but it was clear that there were some hurt feelings and resentments about how Uncle had planned the future.

On Sunday we went up Biamanga (Mumbulla) and performed the particular ceremonial sequence for the mountain. Terry Hayes had a role here because his family is Mumbulla. We then went down to the pools and falls at the foot of the mountain to send off another portion of Uncle's ashes. It was a really strong moment because the ashes entered a little whirlpool and stayed there for some minutes. That old man was always reluctant to leave a ceremonial event.

That final part at the falls was conducted in silence too, and I'm sure everyone there was conscious of the difference between this day and all the other times we had been there when the end of ceremony always culminated in athletic dives and bombs.

The group returning from the pool did so in deep reflection. We joined the rest of Gurandgi and there was a huge sense of relief and satisfaction in having done what the old man had requested in his will.

I'm totally exhausted and deeply, deeply sad, bruised by the months of bickering and missing the presence of the old fella. He changed my life and now it seems lonely living it without him. He gave me and others stern and taxing orders and we are doing our best to live up to his confidence.

More Dramas

I had to get on a plane and get to Redfern and then into the city for the rehearsals of my play *Cutter and Coota* at Hyde Park Barracks.

I felt numb but the cast was vibrant and it is hard to be down when Billy Mack is around. Billy was cast as the cat and various other mischievous things.

After all these years of working on this play and the drama of recent events it was a relief to be distracted by staging it for kids.

Gurandgi pain broke out while I was working on rehearsals and hours were spent trying to find an even, considerate path. I was trying to write new scenes for the play while the phone kept ringing. I needed a break and went to the Rose to have a beer and get some food. It is a strange pub, but people leave me alone there. They are young and completely absorbed in being cool and ordering drugs on their phones. Someone writing in a notebook is as interesting to them as last week's paper on a park bench. They are the generation who will never read a newspaper made from trees.

I was rewriting the play as hard as I could go, jinking and tinkering as the cast rehearsed. I had lunch at the library with an old literary mate, Ailsa Piper, and she told me about a sculpture that she remembered being close to the barracks. I decided I would look for it when I got a chance.

I ran into a whole mob of Blackfellas at the hotel and had breakfast with Tim Harris from Margaret River while we discussed getting our young people educated and employed. When all the young mob went off to the course at the uni I went back to rewriting. I flew home that day and it was a relief to meet only one wombat on the road to the farm. They are slow to make up their mind but once made up it doesn't change. *You* have to change. Nerve-racking on a dark and windy road.

Next morning there was a solid mist in the valley. It was more peaceful than sombre but it did not lend itself to exuberance. I had to pick up wicking beds and ute parts in Bega and meet with old brother Graham Moore, who takes on a lot of the load in the Aboriginal community. His mother is a really important source of the cultural and family information which we all rely on so it's always interesting yarning with Graham.

Knowing how the old wounds and traumas break out in flashes of negative behaviours it must be difficult for him every day. It is difficult for all of us. This morning's mist in the valley and the muted calls of currawongs is my solace and I know that Graham is healed by the view from his verandah at Wallagoot.

I was thinking about all this as I worked on the wicking beds and later stewing feijoas and figs. The day was quite cool so I lit my first fire for the year, feeling sombre, not unhappy, just thoughtful and serious.

I would have watched footy on TV but couldn't find the Tigers so I followed it on my phone. We beat Collingwood, which always proves that God is concentrating.

Lord Howe

Before the fires, before Covid, before we separated, I bought a ticket for Lyn and I to go to Lord Howe Island. Five years later and we decided to go.

The flight to the island was pleasant and so was our simple room. Our first step out the door revealed a Lord Howe Woodhen. Once on the brink of extinction this wonderful bird was saved by eradicating rats and cats.

Lyn and I were both exhausted from our work so we spent a lot of time watching birds over at the jetty beach. There was a White Tern roosting on the branch of a Norfolk Island Pine and we visited it every day around dusk to check on this strange bird. It lays a single egg in small depressions on the branches and the precarious nature of this act tugs at your heart.

We walked about the island as there is only one road and very few cars. There's nowhere to go. But there was history everywhere.

I love museums, especially those with long yarns about boats and lighthouses, so I spent hours wandering slowly from exhibit to exhibit and lost track of time. I could feel my heart and pulse slowing. I was nearly asleep by the time I joined Lyn for coffee.

Lord Howe Island

In the afternoon I had a long snorkel at Ned's Beach and while the coral was quite damaged I was on my own, submerged and drifting. A large blue, pink and purple wrasse decided my mood was her mood and so we dawdled around the reef together, it angling its strange eye toward me and me swivelling my masked eyes toward it. An unusual but relaxed sea couple.

There was a Galapagos Shark, Spangled Drummers and a monk-fish to wonder at as well and I felt quite calm when I knelt at the water's edge to remove my mask. Diving is the best therapy I can imagine and these days I don't do it often enough.

Rambling Ronnie, the tour guide, gave a great talk at the museum and his broad knowledge of geology, history and the natural world gave great food for contemplation. His legs have eliminated his ability to ramble but he brought the island alive with science, which prompted all sorts of conversations in the group listening. Much of that conversation surrounded conserving coral reefs. Humans don't want to lose their planet but we leave its administration in the wrong hands.

Politicians should be chosen from the ranks of those who refuse to apply for the position. We are finding that Gurandgi could benefit from the same principle.

We had a hard walk up the mountain at the north end of the island and then staggered home to cook bolognaise and watch the noddies and terns. The tern had a fish in its mouth to feed its young and it was a privilege to watch an act that began as an epic ocean journey and ended as a scene of silent domesticity.

The bird talk that night at the museum was a classic. Ian Hutton has a lot of information but he does not embellish it with any showbiz. It is a slide show to which he refers with a pointed stick. He dangles the wand toward the tea and biscuits in an indecisive invitation. But he's right, the birds are sufficiently interesting in their own right.

On Friday we walked down to the south end of the island and took the cliff track to watch the Providence Petrels and shearwaters flying about their heathy headland. It is so remote and wild and looks so much like Cape Otway's western headlands. In both places the arcing flights and shrieks of seabirds create their own world of wild ocean, wind and torn cries.

It reminded me of a day on Cape Otway when I went looking for some Aboriginal burials. They were supposed to have been discovered by a fellow planting potatoes. He refused me permission to enter his property so I had to approach it from the ocean side through dunes and swales and tangles of tea tree. I ended up on a sort of mesa with 240-degree views of the ocean, lighthouse and beach.

I could see I had no hope of getting to the property from that direction as there was 3 kilometres of scrub so tangled that Scott Morrison couldn't wriggle out of it.

I looked about this blasted headland and its benches of red waxy sand which I knew had been created by the local mob, the Gatubanoot, as they butchered seals caught on the rock platforms below. The seal oil seeps into the sand and the particles adhere and gradually form a bench, which is more resistant to wind erosion. Further to the east there are old house sites amongst these old butcheries. The archaeologist, Lourandos, worked here many decades ago but his findings found little interest from a nation convinced Aboriginal people were incapable of building a house.

One prominent rock caught my eye and I walked over to it with the hair on the back of my neck creeping and crawling. There was a seat and an anvil created from conveniently arranged blocks of stone. In front of the anvil there was a spray of debitage of chert and silcrete left over from the work of a stone artisan. I didn't have the impertinence to sit in his seat but I cast my eye around the panorama and something shifted within me.

It felt like he had just left to go off to have a drink of water or take a piss and at any moment he might come back and resume his work. He had situated his work station so that he looked out to the ocean, such a mesmeric view and just the right atmosphere for a jeweller's concentration.

I stood there for hours in wonder and honour.

That is what I was thinking as I watched the wheeling and shrieking of the seabirds at Muttonbird Island's wild outpost.

The next morning was spent lazily reading and writing. I swam out to the deep hole at Old Settlement Beach and stooged about with the coral fishes. The Double-header Wrasse is a curious creature with, apparently, not much to do, so you get a good look at him and his manner.

I couldn't help but think of a very vague professor whose brain is too big for his head.

We've had a few meals at Anchorage Restaurant and on our way there this night we saw the supply ship tie up at the jetty and it reminded me of the island trading vessel excitement on King Island when I was a kid. Men and women used to gather at the jetty and watch the unloading while speculating if their sewing machine or ratchet screwdriver was in that box or the other.

And tea and sugar. One month the island ran out of tea and sugar after a particularly bad stretch of weather and people hung around the jetty like addicts outside an injecting room.

While eating our lovely meal at Anchorage, a ute pulled up with the tails of huge fish hanging out the back. They were really big Kingfish and very fresh, their tails still flexing with every lurch of the men carrying them around to the restaurant's cool room.

Once on Skiathos Island while writing my novel, *Fox*, I got up from my hermit desk and realised I hadn't eaten anything but biscuits and cheese for two days. When editing I find it best to read a new book aloud. It is the perfect way to discover a clumsy sentence or a failure of punctuation. I taught a thousand kids the same trick and saw it transform their understanding of the structure of the English language. My fellow tenants may not have been so grateful to hear sonorous English at three in the morning. 'But every now and again the snake remembered where it had been. Might take two hundred years. Maybe forever. But then the waters'd start. Outlet Creek'd fill up. Bring in all the duck and black fish. Pelican'd come. Cod. Mobs of big cod. And then in the sand it remember its old way and push the dust and leaves, nudge the sticks, flick its tongue out. Find its old path, sniffing towards Brmbruk' (McPhee Gribble/ Penguin 1988).

I staggered out looking deranged and took the hill path to a bay where I thought there might be a restaurant. And there it was, perched high above an azure bay. The waiters were hanging around the empty restaurant and fetched me a beer and as I raised the glass to my lips I could hear slap slap slap in the bay below and turned to see a fisherman thwacking squid on the rocks.

I ordered the squid.

On Lord Howe Island order the Kingfish.

We went on the Coral Tour and another wrasse sought out my company. As I snooped into caves and crevices the wrasse shared my interest. When I turned over empty shells the wrasse looked askance at me as if to ask what exactly I had expected to find.

The reef out in the deeper channels is much less bleached and has a richer marine life. I saw a type of dragon fish with long streamers billowing like Elvira Madigan's exotic scarf.

In the afternoon we planned a trip to see the Providence Petrels at the island's southern end. It seemed like a good idea to hire bikes to make the journey but Lyn is not a bike person and her panic was palpable. We fiddled with raising the seat to make it more comfortable for her knees, as we both agreed she'd never make the journey on foot, so, the bike seemed like the best option.

We pedalled in a veering wobble down to the Secret Island and enjoyed the walk through the rainforest. The birds wheeling above us were fascinating but there were a lot of people about so I had a swim amongst the rocks and then reclined in a cave sheltered from the wind. I became intoxicated by the thousands of milling birds and thoughts of their sad history of exploitation by sailors. Hungry sailors need to eat but the Western world seems to have no spiritual handbrake on its consumption.

Time and time again a species will be wiped out. And not just by Europeans, the Māori did it to the Moa and the Easter Islanders cut down all their trees. What did that axeman think as he stood at the base of that final tree?

So, in that Nautilus-shaped cave I thought about the gentleness and conservative nature of Aboriginal spiritual and economic life. How important is that philosophy to the world? It's not a noble savage sentiment, you could think of it as hard-nosed economics. We must not kill the golden goose. The psychology that allows for the last tree to be felled and the golden goose to be killed is an aberration in human history. We must find ways of constraining our greed. Australian Aboriginal people lived as the oldest continuing civilization on Earth while maintaining the fertility of the continent. It wasn't an accident, it was a philosophic adaptation to the nature of resource preservation.

I was grateful to that cave as the waves crept up to my feet and the screech of petrels were a soundtrack to my thoughts, but then we had to walk back to the bikes and wobble our way north. Lyn came to grief and hurt herself but she is a stoic and while she recovered we were visited by Kingfishers sitting on the airport fence.

We got back to the town but will not be investing in bicycles.

We were soon due to fly off the island but the weather was too wild and after a long wait at the airport the flight was called off. The plane from Port Macquarie flew over us but couldn't land and had to turn back for the mainland. Strangely, we met a couple a few weeks later who had been on that plane.

We returned to the accommodation and got our old room back. We were able to check out the petrel feeding its young and watch the unloading and reloading of the *Island Trader*. I'm not sure, but it looks to me that the sewage is removed from the island in tanks. The world's large population develop some unsustainable habits generated by people rich enough to export their shit. And I owned some of the shit.

One more night on the verandah of the pub-type thing opposite the Anchorage as we watched the antics of the Black Noddies, talkative and frenetic birds of good humour.

Eventually we got off the island and travelled home on a series of planes. Soon enough I was feeding ducks at the farm.

Elections and Gardens

The following day I was in Mallacoota at a meeting of the bushfire timber recovery mob who convert fallen trees into timber. I had been hopeful of making use of fallen trees but ours may not be suitable, either too burnt or too small.

The fire recovery continually runs into weird rules and roadblocks and really doesn't warrant the time it takes to apply for assistance. Meanwhile, Terry and Chris had modified the threshing machines to accommodate our grain. Their dedication to finding viable solutions is incredible. We are getting very clean seed now thanks to the method they have perfected to refine our harvests. These are exciting days for everyone at the farm as we develop a machinery process to achieve the results the Old People perfected with completely different tools.

I had a flu but I worked in the gardens and cut wood and then voted in the federal election at Mallacoota and returned home with a feeling of dread. I turned on the TV and gradually the trend of repudiation of a nasty government became clear. Women to the fore.

I worked on the wicking beds and was entertained by the butcher-birds patrolling the ground from the edges of the enclosed gardens. Kookaburras, Mudlarks, ravens, eagles, currawongs all love these vantage points.

My old mate Pete Sands had a serious heart attack but was very lucky to have people staying at his remote Nungatta farm. We have known each other for fifty years, gone fencing together, boating, music, the lot. It rocked me when I heard the news because we'd only just lost Freddy Becker.

The Murnong undergoes a real dieback in late summer but are now shooting again. The lilies never seem to go into recess and we have found that we can get delicious tubers for at least nine months of the year and often twenty to thirty tubers per plant. We harvest five or six times a year without noticeable damage to plant vigour. I think this will be a staple of Australian salads in the future. But will Aboriginal people be allowed in the industry? Or is it just one more dispossession?

Labor had a clear victory in the election and I was expecting the same triumphant gloat of the victor, but Albo hushed the crowd to silence. I thought he wanted a dramatic backdrop to his hubris but, instead, he announced that his government 'would enact the Uluru Statement in full'. I was so taken off guard that I cried, then the great Penny Wong repeated it. What was going on? What had happened to Australia? I was confused, my cynicism about politics cut off at the knees. Suddenly hope seemed possible. I stared at the TV for normal service to resume but the first statement by the new government was about Aboriginal people. It was a new dawn.

New dawns can turn into hot and blustery days but as I write this ten months later the government wrestles its way toward a date for a constitutional acknowledgement of Aboriginal people, and in Victoria the stoic elders of the Treaty group edge ever closer to a treaty, which will cause a cascade of states to follow. We might have treaty, constitutional change and sovereignty within the space of a few years. I hear, and understand, the views of those who think that altering the colonial constitution is not the way to forge change, but I cannot find it in me to reject this offer of a new start for Australia.

The result will be known by the time this book is published and, while I am very anxious, I feel that Australia wants to change its mind about its identity. We don't need to ditch Vegemite and Southern Cross windmills but we must recognise the shovel of Australian history that we chose to call a garden trowel. There will be challenges and bruises in the future but at least it won't be the niggardly past we have endured.

Language on Fire

The fog hung over the valley in totally still air and within the silence of this gauzy world I worked on the wicking gardens. I shovelled scoria in and started to build up the soil with Kangaroo Grass straw and fish frames.

Noel and Trish arrived in the afternoon after a tour of Victoria. That pair were badly knocked around by the fire. Losing the house and all Noel's grandfather's traditional implements was hard enough, but it is their souls for which I fear. There is a kind of lethargy and immovable dread that hangs like vapour.

They enjoyed their travel away from their burnt block and seemed a little revived and, while it is a relief to see them more relaxed, it is also important for Black Duck Foods because their solid commitment and experience has got us through some very trying times.

The next day we had a big yarn with all the people on the farm and Noel's contribution was invaluable. It is wonderful to see Aboriginal men deep in conversation about cultural matters. When I first came to the farm I found an old plastic Coca-Cola table in the shed. It was my only table for eighteen months and as we sat around it for morning teas we started writing language words on its surface as a memory aid. Noel has a lot of language so, when he's here, we're constantly referring to the table and comparing northern Yuin language to the south. We add to and adjust the list and it has helped my ability to remember language.

I don't find it easy to learn language but seeing it every day has helped a lot and visitors can look from bird or beast to the table to find out its language name, a great way to build relationship with Country.

Thursday was busy with collecting more scoria for the gardens and then a Twofold Aboriginal Corporation board meeting and when I returned saw a big golden dingo zig-zagging across the burnt patch on Lightning Ridge.

The Black Duck meeting was still in process with jokes and laughter but was halted momentarily when an Owlet-nightjar's call distracted us. We can never take these visitations for granted but we had to get back to Black Duck business, working out our accommodation packages for guests. We are trying to give people a good experience while not making too many demands on our staff members.

The lyrebirds had been really loud and active over the last few weeks as the autumn weather gets hold of the country. Lyn commented that 'the mornings are uplifted with the ringing calls of lyrebirds.'

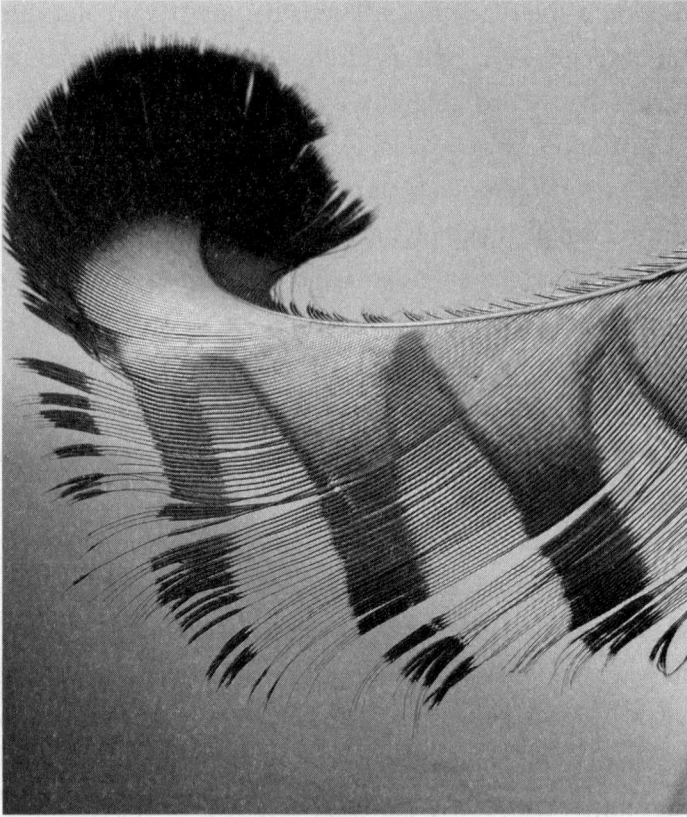

Lyrebird feather

Their calls really do take over at this time of year and their increased activity is a delight. They run like grand dames lifting their skirts to bustle off the road as we approach.

The tracksides are constantly scarified by their claws as if tended by constant gardeners. They and the bandicoots turn fallen leaves and branches into soil and are very important contributors to tilth. The absence of bandicoots and the decline of lyrebirds is a result of predation by cats and foxes and the removal of that daily tilling has seriously impacted Australian soils.

The fellas have been preparing food to send to the CSIRO. We are testing for nutritional information and to make sure there are no harmful properties in the prepared food. Foods already tested have shown protein levels three times that of the European equivalent and no harmful compounds. This is time-consuming work but essential if we are to sell our food with confidence.

I got poor old *Nadgee* to Eden for repairs to some old flood and storm wounds but fortunately the electrical problem that has been plaguing me was found to be faulty battery leads. I got her in the water and she runs as sweet as a bun. Such a relief to be back amongst the riverland's secret tunnels and bays.

On Saturday 28 we went to the reopening of the Genoa footbridge which had been destroyed in the fires. Wilma Becker opened it in memory of her brother, Freddy. Genoa is still hurting from what they see as CFA neglect during the fires and CFA members like Lyn and I have been getting the silent treatment.

The horror of that fireball and the realisation that lives could have been lost has burnt itself into brains like a brand. None of us can forget it.

On the morning of the fires I was on my way to help Dave Severs, publican and postman, because I knew he would fight but I didn't get that far because there were already fires at the Becker family houses at Maramingo Creek.

Ronnie Becker's tank stand was on fire and I put it out with buckets of water from the dam but then I noticed fire was under Ronnie's house too. As I was working on it, Freddy turned up and we crawled under the house to rake out the fire. Freddy was such a good bloke and we've known each other for fifty years so we were tossing news and jokes over our shoulders as we worked.

When we went to check on Freddy's house, I was touched to hear him call each of the chooks by name as he let them out of the chook house. Ronnie and Freddy took off to check on Wilma's house, the old family mill cottage and I went across the highway to see what had happened to Ron and Jacqui, the couple who ran the local boarding kennels.

We knew they had built a fire shelter from an old shipping container and Ronnie held out no hope for them. It took hours for me to cut my way in to their place. There were trees down everywhere. I don't know that I have ever seen the results of a hotter fire.

At last I reached the kennels and listened for the sounds of dogs. It was holiday season, there were usually thirty dogs there. Silence. I walked on in the deepest dread I have ever felt.

The kennels were silent and the front part of the residence had disappeared but in the other part I could see a light on. I stared at it in disbelief. I crept up to the house in real fear of what I expected I would find.

Then I thought I saw someone move in the kitchen. I knocked on the door and Jacqui opened it and I just grabbed her and picked her up. Strangely I was angry that she had given me cause for such a fright.

It was wonderful to see them and their house of dogs. I couldn't stay, although I was hanging out to drink tea with live humans, because I had so many more houses to check.

Jacqui and Ron call me the 'coal bringer' because in Celtic lore the first person you see on New Year's Day has to give you a lump of coal.

I left them and went back to Becker's but couldn't find anyone there. Unbeknown to me they were down at the creek trying to fix a broken pump. I thought they had left to work on their sister's place at

Timbillica. In fact, Freddy died of a heart attack as he walked back to the truck to get a shifting spanner.

I left the Maramingo to work on my own place with the saw Freddy had loaned me. 'You'll need this later,' he said, handing me his brand new saw.

Fallen trees blocked the Wallagaraugh Road at fifty points and it took me hours to get in to the farm. I kept thinking of Dave and Genoa because I knew they wouldn't let their town burn without a fight.

I also knew they'd get no help. The highway was completely blocked and CFA policy wouldn't risk a tanker on the Mallacoota-Genoa Road. The brigade has a responsibility to its volunteer force but in the heat of the fires that is not what residents think. They are looking for a big red truck with hoses and water.

Those trucks never came to Genoa and I know how that felt because later in the fires I was begging for trucks to help me with fires at neighbouring properties but there were none who could help. That feeling of abandonment is not easy to forget no matter how many good reasons there are not to send trucks into risky situations.

Dave, Lars, Big Dennis, Rob and others did an incredible job at Genoa. There were houses lost but, apart from Freddy, no lives. Dave told me later that he saw a fireball take off from a hill 3 kilometres north-west of the town and land a further 3 kilometres to the south. It exploded on a granite ridge, which narrowly missed farms and houses. I can still see that bomb site from my place.

It seemed to me that a fire truck located in the centre of the Genoa township with access to the water tank (which, incredibly, was padlocked shut) would have survived the fire's approach and then been available to help residents after the fire had passed. It's all academic now but I know that sense of being totally alone and I know the feeling of begging for assistance that doesn't come.

I reckon I had thirty packs of bottled water, half a ton of sugar lollies, toilet paper and 'out of use-by' goods dumped at the farm after the fires, but nobody came to help and later nobody asked what I really needed.

Toward the end of the fires, I remember sitting slumped on my verandah trying to regain the energy to go and monitor a fire in the south valley when I saw a posse of people in serious uniforms approaching from the river. Very polite, very well-equipped and all from the Department of Agriculture and, as I say, uniforms so crisp that March Flies who landed on them were cut in half.

Fire fighting set up

'What do you need?' they asked. 'Five hundred kilo of Kangaroo Grass seed,' was my reply. 'Oh, we can't give you that, but we've brought you some water and lollies.' I remembered my mum and dad's insistence on politeness at all times and it is the only thing that saved me from beginning to bellow like a lunatic.

Over the next few weeks I continued to keep the fires under control with the help of neighbours, and every time I came back there was a new slab of water, packets of lollies and wise instructions on how to fight fires and keep hydrated.

Some of the aid that arrived for the brigade included trousers where the zips were in reverse, out-of-date breakfast spreads that no one would buy. Even the grandkids refused to eat them. I have a peaked cap, fridge magnet, water bottle and a biro from every Victorian government department, biros that last only four days but have cheery instructions to drink water in hot weather, fridge magnets with advice so oblique and in such small print that they look like a canary has walked across them.

I hated seeing brand-new utes coming up my driveway with the trays crammed with trash, the calling cards of the charitable. It took me weeks to get back into town, or more particularly, feel like going into town, and when I did, I had whispered conversations with people relaying their experience of the most traumatic time of their life. And they wanted to talk to me and I was desperate to talk to them because we knew we had been there, we had seen it.

No water thanks, no chocolate bullets if you don't mind, thanks for the back-to-front trousers that you knew you couldn't sell, but really, what I want is to talk to someone who was there, someone who I didn't know was alive or dead. Everybody in town has been changed by the fires but next time I hope government agencies go beyond handing out trinkets.

We had some of Australia's richest people going on television to offer the world when all the town actually got was the heart thumping benefactor's thirty second media grab. Not a cracker. Thanks, rich man.

Many Mallacootians were great, but the local church minister, Jude, was unstoppable in the recovery. I have become averse to the sanctimony and patrimony of the church but there is none of that with Jude. She rolled up her sleeves and opened up her big practical heart. She made an enormous difference to how the town rebounded. To me that is Christianity, dirty hands, clean heart.

A lot of people were full of real sorrow for our district and, in the aftermath, we got some free concerts. I dragged myself to one where Kylie Minogue arrived but didn't sing. The crowd was beyond caring. The mood was not, entertain us, let's have fun, but rather, this is my town and I've come to be with my people. I spent the whole concert sitting on the grass listening to an old mate, an Australian music legend, tell me he was dying of cancer and how disappointed he was. Not complaining, just pissed off.

There was beer there and I'm usually an enthusiast, socially excitable, but I chewed on half a can as if it were ashes.

I went along to another free, 'cheer Mallacoota up' gig at the golf club on Sunday 29 May. It was the Australian Youth Orchestra. They had already been to the school to teach the kids and now they were here to play for us. They were incredible. The golf club bar was full of golfers in 'nearest to the piss mode' but in the next room we listened enthralled.

I've never been closer to an orchestra in my life. I could see their fingers press down strings, surreptitiously wipe the wind instruments and turn the pages of the score for their neighbouring musician. It moved me to tears that they would come and do this in our tiny town. I never expected to see anything so generous. And not one offer of water in a plastic bottle or a crateload of chocolate bullets.

I have to admit that many Mallacoota residents were very grateful for the lollies, but I'm a curmudgeon and Mum said never to accept lollies from strangers.

The memories of the fire are stubborn and very, very private. They don't go away and I don't think my energy has fully returned. I got a whack in the eye from the whippy branch of a burnt tree at some point in the fire and didn't realise for a few days that my eye was distended and black. Happens when you don't wash! I'm still getting treatment for the fluid behind the eye. Yes, it's hard to forget.

After the bridge commemoration day, I had to fly to Sydney to work at a school in Mosman and that night I did a gig with Charlie Arnott on food sovereignty at the local church. Hardly ever been colder than in that old church. Were they Presbyterians? But we raised some money for Black Duck Foods thanks to the enthusiasts at the Fairlight Butcher.

I was completely drained at the end and couldn't order dinner at the airport hotel for fear of breaking out in a stutter. Back home at the farm it was very cold. I slashed alongside the track out to Wallagaraugh Road to try and constrain the regrowth that has burgeoned since the fires and then Mook took over. He said it was so cold in the paddocks that tears were coursing down his face. Happy days on the farm, eh? But we just have to work if the weather is even tolerable. I love the fellas for never complaining.

Winter

Wattle flower

It's winter now. The days shorter, the weather more grim, the sunny mornings more fleeting. It is the time for the spiky white flowering wattle to bloom and tell us the fish are coming upstream.

Light in the Forest

The forest surrounding the farm has been logged several times, often illegally. The bigger trees are around forty years old but now with masses of younger trees which grew after the 2019 fires.

The old Aboriginal forest, as encountered by the first Europeans, was mostly dominated by massive trees with grassland as the understory. The current Australian forest has smaller trees and a canopy more vulnerable to wildfire.

We are attempting to thin our forest so that we can get back to around seventeen large trees per hectare, basing the density on old photos and colonial drawings of the district.

We began by selecting a section of mixed forest and reducing the canopy by about 25 per cent. The logs were used to construct sheds and fences but some were used to make swales to slow the movement of water across the block. Grasses returned immediately and now that we have observed the change we are about to reduce the number of trees by a further 25 per cent.

After Uncle Max's passing we joined the stems of a double trunked tree within this forest as a memorial. In seventy years it will begin to resemble the tree near Brogo through which Uncle was invited to pass. Within 300 years it will be roughly the size of Uncle's Brogo tree.

In 2021, seventy-five Yuin men performed ceremony at Uncle's old tree and in creating another ceremonial site we hope similar events may happen again at Yumburra. There is already evidence of a dance ground and scar trees on the property and the discovery of the Yumburra axe in 2023 at the site of our new grain-processing shed was proof that we were not the first Yuin people who worked on the site. We know that we're on the Dangar (damper or bread) storytrack so that axe is part and parcel of the grain cycle.

Since the fires of 2019 the bush is dominated by Black Wattle and Hop Goodenia so thick that if you surprise a lyrebird or wallaby on the track, they have to run in a mad scamper ahead of you because it is simply impossible to penetrate this regrowth. The flammability of this stage of regrowth is of great concern to us. It will generate a fire far hotter and more dangerous than the 2019 fire.

We have to rethink our forest and national park management but it is essential to properly resource the forest authorities if we want to reduce these threats. Every region is different, so the plan needs to be flexible enough to incorporate forest diversity. That will require good science, Aboriginal participation, adequate budgets and boots on the ground. Fewer fridge magnets and water bottles and more Aboriginal employment.

I was visited on June 2 by a lovely bloke from Melbourne University who wanted to talk forest thinning. I took him on a tour and showed him our sites … and never heard from him again. Similarly with an agricultural messiah who was full of grand plans for our farm. Gone without trace.

Tyre kickers visit the farm all the time, enthralled by our efforts, but seemingly unable to gain leverage over their department, move to another job or move on to the next dream.

We are talking forest plans, which need at least thirty years to show their merit while Australia plans within a three-year electoral cycle. We must think further into the future and back the plans produced by thought and research. We know that the fires of 2019 will return with increased frequency, finding ways to make the national forests less dangerous is crucial to the national safety response to global warming.

The season became cooler with quilts of mist at dawn and the currawongs and bowerbirds hungrier, so Bell's food bowl was watched carefully and subject to lightning raids. Bell is too mild and creaky to object these days.

That night I was sitting around the BBQ fire, contemplating the slow arrival of sunset and a lovely cold, Dark Emu, when I was invaded by hundreds of Fork-tailed Swifts and perhaps Needletails. I find them difficult to distinguish.

They visit only three or four times a year and always precede a weather change. The bird travels between here and Siberia at speeds of around 125 kilometres per hour. When they pass you it is with the sound of a text being sent. Woosh.

I stood up to watch the arrival but then they started coursing the house paddock and flicked past me at knee height, war heads the size of falcons. I was surrounded by these missiles, too scared to move, hoping that their dexterity would preserve both them and me.

Decades ago, Lyn and I were gifted a swift damaged in a collision with a car, so I had a right to be nervous. We built up the bird's strength by feeding it insects but there was no way we could tell if it had the energy to fly.

The birds can sleep on the wing apparently and need Himalayan-style cliff faces to launch themselves. We lived close to the abrupt cliffs of the Otway Coast which greet the winds from the violent weather systems of the Southern Ocean.

We watched the bird carefully for improvement, not sure how to assess its recovery as it seemed reluctant to drink. When I had the farm at Maramingo, across the river and over the range, my neighbours were the Beckers, a timber milling family. They were avid bird watchers and naturalists and, while they didn't do much formal schooling they spent a lot of time learning the bush.

One day they photographed a swift drinking from the Maramingo Creek. The birds swooped in low to the water and dropped their lower mandible so that their beak spiked the surface and sprayed water into their mouths. The Beckers were told that their photograph was the first showing a swift drinking in Australia.

It was a remote life in that part of the world in the 1950s and often the postman-cum-butcher couldn't deliver meat to them for weeks at a time. They regaled me with recipes for Wonga Pigeon, Satin Bowerbird and King Parrot. Another crusty local says that lyrebird is the best roast he has ever had. Mallacoota had an old fisherman grace their streets for sixty years but when he died the local Wonga population trebled.

These pigeons run into our windows occasionally and we are quick to scoop up the prize and pluck it fresh. Wonga pie is a favourite meal, unsustainable for 26 million people but very tolerable when the human population was 1-2 million and the totemic system ensured no food was over-harvested.

Anyway, back at the Swift Hospital, information on caring for these injured birds was non-existent so we were unsure what to do for such a wild and psychologically inaccessible creature. They almost never encounter humans except as a cowering blur.

Lyn and I used to take tours of the Cape Otway Lighthouse and its white bulk was used as a sighting board for swifts hunting insects. They would rocket toward the light before veering away at the very last second much to the consternation of the tourists.

But what to do with the swift in our care? We bit the bullet and carried it out to the highest cliff on the coast when a northwesterly was blowing hard and we threw the swift into the wind. It dropped to the rocks below like a brick. We stood in silence looking out to sea.

Wildlife shelters experience an inordinate amount of death. Tourists brought us koalas, often the same one, kingfishers, echidnas, joeys, eagles, owls; the courtyard saw them all. We named the Gang-gang Cockatoo Clark, because that's all it said.

We were told it would never fly again as it had a complex break in its wing. We used to take it out every morning so that we could lift it into a tree on a surf rod. At dusk Clark was very happy to climb on to the rod and accompany us back to the house to be fed sunflower seeds.

He would ride on our shoulders when we escorted Jack down the track to meet the school bus. He needed an escort because, like me, he hated school. Whenever Clark rode on Jack's shoulder he took a piece out of his ear. Jack soon tired of Clark even though the bird's fame was known in several states. He even took phone calls from one ten-year-old admirer. 'Hullo Clarkie,' Izzie would say and Clark would always agree. 'Clark,' he would reply. Short conversations but deep in meaning.

A magpie eventually stabbed Clark in the eye and killed him. Just one more reason to hate Collingwood!

Oil spills meant an influx of penguins and a call out to local fishermen for pilchards and sprat. The little birds are an incredibly smelly animal. Washing and grooming the birds so that they didn't ingest the oil was a constant trial even though the little toddlers were such vibrant company.

Vets told us that the trick would be to get any survivors to swim again because they need that action to lubricate their feathers with their oil. Swimming them at Point Franklin was a delight as they loved to flick around the rockpools like underwater darts. When tired they would waddle onto the rocks and head straight to us. Home to the warmth and constant supply of fresh pilchard.

Our first penguin did this for months even though the pool had an outlet to the sea. One day she did her normal circuit and vigorous cleaning and then exited the pool by the entrance she had avoided on every other occasion. She was gone.

We watched her for minutes riding the swell as she looked out to sea, but then she dived and we never saw her again. She became part of the great Southern Ocean again, leaving us looking at the black slap of wintry waves.

Following the Whale

Yaraan Bundle and her parents asked us to join their whale celebration at Warrnambool. It's a ten-hour drive but Yaraan's mob came to our Yuin whale ceremony about five years ago and for Bobbo, her dad, it was a return to Country and a chance to unite the whale stories along the coast. Yaraan had received a whale story at birth and that piece fitted into ours like the piece of a jigsaw. Yuin have been joining pieces of story from around the country over the last decade so these occasions are vital for our cultural survival.

There is a long way to go in that unity but the Warrnambool celebration is one of those opportunities. Terry Hayes came with us and we all had breakfast with my niece's children and then went on to the festival.

It was freezing cold but we were warmed by the fact that Yaraan and her mum, Vicki Couzens, spoke in language about the journey of the whale along the south coast. I have worked with Vicki on language for over twenty years and before that Vicki's father, Ivan, provided some of the best advice I have ever been given.

In conversations with Uncle Ivan and Uncle Banjo I learnt the horrible history of Western Victoria but, despite that horror, both men were so positive and light of heart it was an inspiration just to be in their company. Uncle Ivan told me about the bear traps that await any Aboriginal person who attempts to make positive change. So many people want Aboriginal people to be totally dependent on white society, supplicants of the colony.

The Liberal and National parties' refusal to back the Voice and constitutional recognition were just the latest in this refusal to acknowledge Aboriginal people as the First People of the continent.

Being at the whale ceremony was a commitment to the action Uncle Ivan fought for all his life. He and his brother Rocky were invited to play for Hawthorn in the AFL, but one night staying in a hotel where the other players drank until early morning in an atmosphere of near riot convinced them the world of AFL was not for them.

The presence of those two men was very close as we drove through the battlefields of Western Victoria on our return.

Back home, the day dawned bright and frosty. Bowerbirds and Crimson Rosellas assembled on the lawn in front of the house as if attending a lore meeting. They fed there all morning but I was unsure what they were eating. The habits of birds and their concentration on their lives is always entrancing.

That night a wild storm rocked the poor old house but I delighted in a fine mist of rain chilling my face as it fretted at the fly wire of my bedroom window.

Vagrant Jesus

I had to go to Sydney for a gig at the Art Gallery of NSW to yarn with Badger Bates. I used the journey to read books on Aboriginal astronomy as part of the research for a new Magabala book on the night sky.

Wes Shaw was organising the event. Wes is Gurandgi and it was my first chance to see him at his quiet and respectful work. After the event Badger was keen to have a meal and a drink, which sounded very appealing, but Wes was my lift home and he wanted to get back to his family. Once back at Kings Cross I had two lovely schooners while looking out onto that mad and vibrant street.

I love the Kings Cross Hotel but, while the view from it is colourful and lively, and I never tire of that vibrance, I do grieve for the struggle of many of those lives. Next morning, I had a sad breakfast in the dirtiest cafe I have seen in years. Home of the desperate.

I had to wait to do a job for Craig Reucassel, the face of the ABC program *War on Waste*, so I filled it in by trying to see *Mystery Road*, but the programming was indecipherable for an old fella from the river, so I ended up watching *Children of the Mist* and haven't stopped thinking about it since. The whole idea of camera as voyeur is troubling but the revelation of life was transfixing.

I remembered my old friend, Ailsa Piper, telling me about an interesting sculpture at St Mary's Cathedral but her directions were quite hopeless which may be why she follows Sydney Swans. Eventually I found the church and the sculpture beside it. A man is shrouded in a rough blanket while sleeping on a park bench. His crudely punctured feet poke out from beneath the blanket. The vagrant Jesus.

The intent of the sculpture is so profound but the acceptance of it by the church is evidence that the Christian ethic is alive. I sat with the sculpture for an hour. Not one of the people who walked past seemed to notice it. Was it too realistic, or too common to be interesting? If all Christians had the heart of the sculpture and the generosity of this church, I would attend every Sunday.

Ailsa's instructions were so vague that I had to visit three churches before I found the vagrant Christ and so had hours of restful stained-glass reflection. Tourists were snapping on their phones and chatting happily while the devout tried to pray in silence. For what did they pray? Departed family members, the sick, the lonely? That the church never again takes Aboriginal children from their parents?

My time with Christ the Vagrant was solemn and bleak as I sat with blown pigeons, swirling paper, heedless pedestrians and my own gloom.

Sydney was blustery and lonely and in this mood it was a long, slow walk back to the Cross. While I had a peculiar meal at the Kings Cross Hotel, Lyn was visiting the farm to feed my ducks. There were so many dead trees after the fires that storms produce a shower of falling branches. It is very dangerous and so I worried about Lyn on that long bush road.

I was reminded of the hazardous climb up Mount Goongerah that Uncle Max had made me vow to complete. After three journeys through the clashing spears of that incinerated forest the task is still not quite finished. We wait for a calm day but they are not common on the mountain; which is exactly why Uncle needed us to inspect it for him.

I did the interview with Reucassel at the Powerhouse Museum the next day. He is an earnest man but quite distant, maybe just distracted, from carrying the burden of capitalism's waste.

The weather was so wild in Gippsland that when I returned to the farm I was blocked by dozens of fallen trees. Just like the fires, but colder and darker, and just like the foreboding of Goongerah.

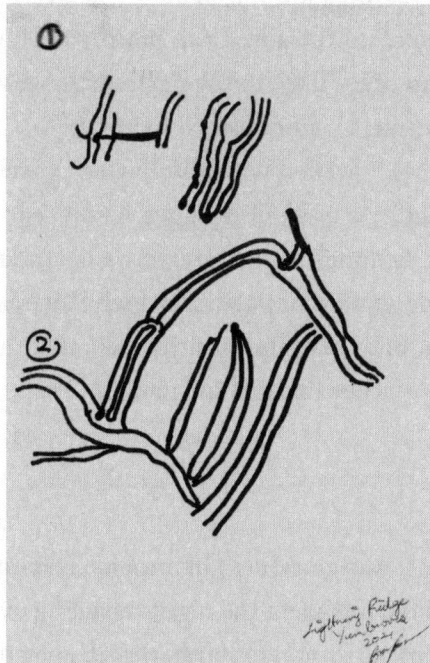

Wood Grub lines

The next day was also very cool and my old mate Graham Sheil arrived. I met Graham through publishing his stories in *Australian Short Stories* magazine over a few decades.

He is a great raconteur and, like me, a bit of an outsider in the literary world. He writes about life from the point of view of his travels to wild places and his stories are rich with culture and character. I could never understand why his work was not more popular.

Once he cajoled me into visiting the Irian Jaya highlands. He liked the wildest places but the Indonesian government didn't like that I was a writer, so my only way of entering was through the high ridges of Papua New Guinea. They still didn't like me, but in the higher country there are few Indonesians as they are averse to the cold, so we managed our journey with only occasional interrogations and commands by army and police.

That journey requires a book of its own. My novel *Ruby-Eyed Coucal* recounts some of the adventure but my most vivid memory is of being sung from one village to the next where we would be met by villagers singing us in. Country joined by song.

On occasions we travelled with the Papuan guerilla group OPM as that was the only way some villages would admit us, so afraid were they of the Indonesian authorities. The Indonesians do not understand the Indigenous population which Australia allowed them to invade in 1962, but Australia is in just as much ignorance of the Indigenous territory they invaded in 1788.

That night, 15 June, was glorious. The moon, Grandmother Yedding, rose well before dusk and spent the night travelling over the old farmhouse in an arc from north-east to south-west. By dawn she was looking in my west window, a wonderfully calm and reassuring presence.

There was a hard frost overnight; totally expected given the still, bright air of the night.

Grace wanted to film on the lake so I took her in *Nadgee* down to Dead Finish on the Top Lake and drew the whole lore of the lake in the sand of the beach. Only one person lives on that part of the lake, the scientist Barbara Triggs, who wrote the definitive book on animal tracks, scats and signs. Much of her knowledge came from studies of animal footprints on this deserted beach.

Barbara lived an incredibly isolated life at Dead Finish but her deserted beach was her manuscript. I knew her husband, Alan Triggs, a decorated British fighter pilot. I often saw his yacht anchored off their house, mirrored perfectly by the still lake. It remains for me one of those images for me of the perfect paradise.

I often fish and prawn in the Top Lake and I am always conscious of Barbara's watchfulness and possessive care.

Alan and I often enjoyed a beer in the Genoa pub in the seventies when we both came in to get our mail. He and I and Arthur and Dulcie used to yarn about local history in long, convoluted conversations.

Arthur and Dulcie, old residents of the district, feature in a few of my stories, one in particular, 'Splitter', which appeared in my first collection, *Night Animals*. In fact, conversations in the Genoa Hotel would account for more than half of the stories in *A Corner Full of Characters*.

On the way back from the lake, Grace and I called in to Lyn's and lit her fire because I knew she'd be home late from getting her car serviced in Bega. The air at four was already steely with the prospect of another frost.

The moon rose as a huge ball and the sky was freckled with crimped wool clip clouds, a sure sign of cold air arriving.

When I came out onto my verandah in the middle of the night, Grandmother Yedding was a lonely sailor high in the sky and

Koon ar rook (Wood Ducks), complained at my disturbance and Birran Durran Durran (Spur-winged Lapwing), fretted in the valley for the same reason. Man.

The morning was cool and Rosco and I went up the hill to cut a leaning tree I've had my eye on since the fires. That one tree will provide most of my firewood for this winter. After finishing that job we went across to Lyn's and cut up some of the timber that dropped around her place during the fires. We were able to fill her woodshed too. Grace, Rosco and I had dinner at Lyn's place and I watched Richmond beat Carlton. I'm a hopeless sport fanatic; I much prefer it to war.

I got a call to say that Aunty Koonka had passed away the following day. I got to know her family when I was helping compile the Wathaurong language dictionary in Geelong. Her family had been shattered by the Stolen Generation and, as a result, Koonka's heritage was largely unknown.

I encouraged the family to follow the little information Koonka had and the hospital records from where Koonka's own children had been stolen. It's a shocking story and the callous indifference of the people who were paid to care should be known to all Australians. This is our country, and our country needs to own the heritage of dispossession of the First Nations. It is a painful journey but it is not a lie.

Decades later, one of Koonka's daughters wrote her family history under the supervision of the Aboriginal writer Tony Birch. Finding Koonka's Aboriginal family was a triumph but the realisation that the Old People had been waiting for a male relative of just the right skin showed how vital it is to search for family, painful as it always is.

I don't know anyone for whom it was unalloyed joy and for some it was achieved along with deep sadness and loss. This pain is why Aboriginal people need a Voice, so that we can ask the difficult questions rather than be met with an invitation to assimilate and disappear. We want to know our families, one of the most basic human impulses.

The colonial hindrances are real and contemporary. The right-wing press have been giving me a kicking and the mates of a previous non-Aboriginal employee are blocking and disrupting our progress simply because we disagreed with their opinion on how best to support Aboriginal employment.

Black Duck's central motivation is to employ Aboriginal people. It is depressing that it seems such a revolutionary idea and, even more depressing, that some think only white people can do it.

In the middle of this issue I was rung by a journalist wanting to know what I would ask my right-wing adversaries if I ever met them. I said that I would ask them if they took milk and sugar in their tea. My answer seemed to displease the journalist but what I meant was that we need civil conversation about our disagreement rather than one long adversarial slanging match.

Around this time I tried to install a satellite so I could watch football, but to no avail. Reception is hopeless in this area and satellite dish installation is surely the job of professionals not broken down half-back flankers.

Lyn was due to come over for tea but the slipperiness of the track thwarted her. The constant drizzle has made the uphill sections of the track quite difficult but we're hoping to get more gravel on to them soon.

On Saturday 18 I flew up to Brisbane to do a gig at Northey Street Farm. There were good panel discussions and a whole mob of Blackfellas wanted to yarn about their food dreams, particularly employment and sovereignty. I have to remind myself that the attacks of the right-wing, meant to unsettle and divide us, do not separate good people from good people. It was a greatly reassuring day.

I also met Melissa Lucashenko there, author and Miles Franklin winner. We've been mates since long before the Liberal Party had a policy designed to benefit Aboriginal Australians. That is, decades.

I am not a social person. I grew up lonely in lonely places and loved it. I ran into Melissa in Adelaide one night before the city's writers festival, and she's more socially reticent than me. We had dinner together. Kindred cranky spirits.

The night of the Northey Street Farm's annual Winter Solstice Festival I stayed in a hotel which had better security than Junee prison; and the security of that prison I could take as a specialty subject on *Hard Quiz*. There was no restaurant open within cooee so I ate a packet of chips from a vending machine. Next morning, I tried hard to find a place that sold food and ended up eating something warmed in the glass cabinet of the BP servo.

I caught a ride out to the airport with a sister girl and mate of Melissa's. Both of us were starving and suffering from enclosure. Aboriginal incarceration rates are higher than people realise! What did we do wrong?

I flew to Melbourne and saw Marnie and family and ate a home-cooked meal with the babble of family life barely penetrating the fog of my weariness.

I picked up my new Subaru and drove home but I only got as far as Lyn's place at Gipsy Point. The car I sold to Jack a decade ago began to decline and he wanted mine. I sold it to him but had to wait six months to get another one because everybody was buying cars and toilet paper during Covid. I wanted an electric car but Subaru seem to be refusing to make one and, in any case, country distances are still a challenge for them.

I can't believe that current electric car makers all have different charging systems. Men have learnt nothing since the big fellas decided to make uncomplimentary railway gauges in NSW and Victoria. Where was the woman to say, 'Lads, put it away, your ego is not as important as a single gauge between Australia's two biggest cities.' No, state rights are essential for the survival of the male and it's important for them to show who is boss!

We had two days of conference up at Yambulla to discuss Aboriginal food production and we smoked all the attendees in a dignified ceremony. Nathan, Terry and Rosco did it beautifully. We talked about cool burning but none of the guests had seen a cool burn so we lit one up.

Terry lights a fire

'You won't get it to burn today,' the experts insisted but of course the fire crept in a steady pace across the grassland. 'But now you've burnt the young grass,' the experts chirped, but I just swept my hand across the burnt section to remove the ash and there below were the unburnt shoots of young grass.

Next morning, as we talked esoteric data theory, kangaroos descended on the burnt patch to nibble the exposed green shoots; a perfect example of why and how we burn. Australians will learn a lot in coming decades from such demonstrations.

Not all fire, however, is good fire, so the country has to be assessed very carefully to know the best time to burn and where. Burning country just because you can is not good science or culture.

When I came home I saw Cattle Egrets interacting with the bulls at Genoa Farm. I remember the first year they arrived in the Genoa valley in the seventies. They'd never been seen so far south so their sudden arrival was a mystery and a joy. I love the casual relationship between the two vastly different creatures.

Blackfellas

I had a long day of travel on 25 June to do an opening for an event run by David Gough in Tasmania. Years ago, David asked me to look at some stone etching of his people in the north of the state. His struggles to represent the culture moved me deeply and I was keen to support his event.

There were young black musicians playing at the opening and I was proud of their expertise. Patrick Churnside was a participant and I have been following his work on the Burrup Peninsula for decades.

I have had long interest in the Burrup art and Patrick is one of those at the forefront of its care. It is complicated because mining interests have built the local Aboriginal cultural centre and part of the community feel obliged not to criticise the number and placement of fertiliser factories being built close to the art galleries. It's none of my business except that I have general concerns for the culture.

It seems grotesque to treat the millions of stone etchings like that, risking their oblivion with chemical erosion, but it is a very hard place for Aboriginal people to negotiate. Anyway, my job was to be in Wynyard supporting David Gough and his community. It was a terrific evening but the travel eroded me and I went to bed early.

Lyn had come over to light my fire and prepare dinner which was a lovely thought. It was great to be home. I have two swallows who roost on the back verandah light every winter. They make a terrible mess but they are such good friends I cannot deny them the shelter.

I have built them a little shelf below the light to catch most of their droppings. It is a patented SSS; Swallow Shitting Shelf.

While I was writing this, an old mate, Michael Drake, passed away. At that very moment a swallow flew in through his open door and no amount of encouragement could get it out. When Lyn heard she asked Michael's wife June, 'Did Michael like swallows?' June's jaw dropped and she replied, 'He did, he spoke to them for hours every day.'

The next morning, Kuboka (Grey Shrikethrush) songbird was very hungry. I feed it a little cheese from time to time in winter. It seems grateful and never asks at any other season. The Jacky Winters' chiming voice is a feature during winter as they come close to the house gardens. I revel in their company and miss them when I'm away.

A mob of us went to Merimbula to support a Koori film, *The Lake of Scars*. It was a good film and presented by that great heart, the late Jack Charles. Jack has never been anything but kind and supportive toward me. We often ended up walking together in rallies or talking in a corner at Blackfella events. He was a great man, loved by everyone who knew him. Those who overcome adversity are often particularly tolerant and supportive of others. It is their natural instinct.

It was a long drive home in the dark and we were driving slowly to avoid the kangaroos and wombats. We picked up a dead bandicoot and Lyn was entranced by its sharp little teeth and soft ears.

We usually inspect the pouches of dead marsupials and I remember one time when I found a roo on the Cape Otway Road and extracted a near-naked young. Lyn saw me with the animal and dashed out of the car and her hands were clutching and unclutching to express her need to hold the animal.

It seemed that only a woman could know how to care for the baby. It made me reflect on her visceral reaction to the orphan's needs. She wasn't being rude to me it was just that she couldn't control her impulse.

That kangaroo was raised by us to adulthood through months of dependency and needy temperament. One morning it scratched at the fly wire screen near our bed and left. For a week or so we would find it grazing at dawn close to our window and it would acknowledge us but in a slightly confused manner and eventually it was gone for good.

Windy weather at the farm meant I had to cut obstructions off the track, then we tried to get a burn going in the grassland but it was too damp. That night we had a long Gurandgi meeting to plan our whale ceremony. We hold these meetings at 8 pm, which suits the men with young families, but I am always knackered at the end of the day. My energy has diminished in recent years. But to plan for the whale is an honour and obligation.

We got the fire tanker bogged in what one of the farm workers dubbed Apocalypse Valley after the 2019 fire destruction. We hauled the tanker out with the tractor and tried to make the track safer. It was a bit of a slog in the damp conditions.

That night we had a meeting and dinner with the new Black Duck manager and his family.

Next morning, we performed a Grandfather Sun ceremony so that the manager's daughter could understand our commitment to the great creators. It's a simple ceremony but we love it because it compels us to observe the entire sky and the presence of animals and birds. It settles and focusses us for the rest of the day. On Gurandgi camps we have had up to seventy-five men at Grandfather and the ceremony can take up to two hours. It is bonding and binding.

Lyn's neighbour, Pat Wilkinson, lost her dog, Sheba, on 1 July, so Lyn and I went and buried the dog for her. Pat and her dogs are as close as we are with ours, so it was a stressful event, but allowed Pat to mourn her dog without the pain of handling her burial.

I put another coat of dark blue on the Muslim Gate as the bowerbirds and Wood Ducks gathered on the grass. Are they eating the seeds of Kikuyu Grass and Flickweed? Or insects? As I finished off the gate, twenty-eight Nenak (Yellow-tailed Black Cockatoos) flew over the river.

I worked on an extension to the duck house to prevent their feed from getting wet. It clumps together if it's damp and doesn't drop down into the feeding tray. I worry while I'm away that they will be hungry if it rains.

I took a slow trip down river to have dinner with Lyn and saw thirty-five Binyaroo (Little Black Cormorants). I harvested some lily tubers from the garden. They are lovely at this time of the year and I am sure they will become one of Australia's favourite vegetables. They are clear and snap fresh and delicious.

More cockatoos over the river as a beautiful sunset bled into the sky.

Hens and Dogs and the Pugilism of Kangaroos

Lyn's poor old Tiny Tips, the red hen, died after an incredibly long life. She hadn't laid an egg in years but she refused to give up on her life and struggled up the hill every afternoon during even the hottest weather. She had gravitas, Tiny did.

I shower outside and, at that time of the year, I am able to watch at least three bouts of boxing from groups of young male kangaroos. They try for the higher ground and have begun feinting with the claws on their large feet. It's all hijinks and play before it gets serious.

Those kicks can be deadly as poor old Wangarabell found out when she was a pup. She chased a big roo and it backed into the river and she made the mistake of swimming out to it. The roo grabbed her and ripped her with its hind toe.

We weren't there to see it as we were looking for her on the other side of the house. A neighbour rushed up with the little dog bleeding profusely. A whole flap of skin had come away from her throat to her groin but she had not been disemboweled as often happens.

I slapped the skin back in place and we rushed her up to the vet who sewed her back up like a potato bag. She made a perfect recovery and the only indication of the event were little buttons of scar tissue on her belly. Made of corrugated iron those blue heelers.

Kangaroos are a dangerous animal. Big males will chase each other around the house for hours until one gives up exhausted or wounded and lies panting. The victor goes to the mob of females but is in no fit state to mate until it has recovered.

The defeated usually go off on their own and literally lick their wounds. We watched one old deposed male take to the shade of Lyn's orange tree many years ago and it seemed a lonely, depleted existence after the excitement of living with the mob.

A few months later it was dead and I carried it up to our roo cemetery in the bush behind the tip. Over winter it is common to lose young roos too so there is quite a collection up there for the consideration of Bunjil.

I love the family of roos. If you surprise them the little ones will lean back and appraise you with comic intent. The old males when they rear back like that can look like old masons holding their hands across the furry aprons of their bellies.

Such gentle families

The currawongs are collecting around the house now. There might be thirty or so and they space themselves equidistantly across the grass and stand there stock still before dashing forward a couple of paces to pick something from the grass. This behaviour fascinates me, the social organisation of it, the knowledge of Country.

Of less fascination is their habit of nipping the flowers off the apple tree beside the woodshed. This is an old tree and produces delicious apples if allowed. The currawongs have also developed the habit of stealing the soap from the outside shower. Even if I hide it under a flannel they will dig it out so I have to remember to take it inside.

Wangarabell is terribly restless of an evening these days and does a lot of pacing about and complaining until you sit down to watch the news and then she puts her head in your lap and is asleep instantly. Is she sore or spoilt?

A Beer at Genoa

Late autumn and winter is the time I prune the fruit trees, a real marker of farm rhythms. I also slashed some bracken near the horse paddock and the disturbance of insects delighted the swallows. It was a rainy day while I was on the tractor but quite comfortable on the old Case.

I had been on the farm on my own for days so I contemplated a trip into the big smoke of Genoa to pick up the mail from the pub. I love having a beer with Dave and talking sport and outrageous local scandal. It astonishes me how busy the district can be.

Ken Bridle and Ted (Flat Duck) Dexter were there too. I taught young Ken, but not much, and Ted has only been here thirty years so he has to watch his manners. I really enjoy those quiet beers and the chance to find out what is happening away from my stretch of the river.

The pub is an absolute classic. It was built of pise in the 1920s but a fire destroyed the top floor. It has seen better days but it holds so many memories of music and laughter.

It was the focus of survival during the fires and has been the heart for most community events during its life.

The Genoa auctions used to attract big crowds and blokes you'd only ever see on auction day would creep out of the bush to poke at piles of old tools with a stick, as if in contempt, and then make surreptitious bids because they'd seen a perfectly good shifting spanner amongst the pile. One of those old blokes was me.

You'd often see the same BBQ plate, ratchet screwdriver or patio chair every year. They'd sell so cheaply they'd be irresistible to some people but then when they were viewed in the cold hard light of your own backyard they would reveal themselves as junk. Back to the auction the very next year.

After the auction we'd retire to the hotel and discuss the most notorious purchases. 'He'll never finish that white boat hull. It's cheap alright, but he doesn't know which end of a screwdriver to poke at it.'

Never heard so much wry and good-humoured wisdom.

Painting the Desert

For the last few years Lyn has travelled with a mob of mates on a painting camp in winter. That year they went to Ross River out of Alice Springs and I was allowed to tag along to write.

Poor old Bell can't come but Gurandgi brother Cooma and Alison and young Marlo are going to care for her at Lyn's place.

The long trip to Alice was interrupted by Rex plane delays again so we arrived late. We stayed at the old Ross River Homestead and the mob went off painting every day and I holed up in the room and plugged away at the astronomy book.

One day we all went out to N'Dhala Gorge, which Lyn and I had visited with Jack on our '93 round Australia trip. We travelled in a van the size of a large shoe box but as we fished and swam almost every day it was comfortable enough. It was wonderful to walk the petroglyph trail again and wonder at such a cohesive and gentle philosophic expression of life.

A central theme is the humble caterpillar. I'm always moved by the gentleness of our culture, selecting small things to represent the Earth's power. It shows a completely different attitude to the world and the understanding of human existence within it. No heraldry, no army, no weapons, no butchery, no kings and rooms of gold, but caterpillars and birds that weigh as much as half a dozen cotton balls.

I am entranced by that modesty. Aboriginal people are human with all the same characteristics of the species; love and hate, violence and peace, kindness and cruelty but have an entirely different set of spiritual priorities and governance. I didn't grow up with that knowledge but became exposed to it gradually thanks to an uncle and several generous elders.

It is common for Australians to scoff when I talk about this philosophy but I am certain that, in time, the world will understand the value of viewing existence in this light and, hopefully, ensuring that the originators of this thought can practise it in peace while sharing it with others. Sharing it, not having it usurped.

I am 100 per cent saltwater so this red Country in the Centre is not mine, but being out of Country and the demands of the farm allows me restful anonymity. I sat in the dry riverbed of Trephina Gorge and doodled with a drawing of my three salt rivers. I watched sunsets on rocky outcrops and in this slightly dislocated mood was able to write pages for the astronomy book.

Deb, the artist-organiser, indulged my presence and allowed me to dip in and out of the art projects. I was in awe of how each of the

Lyn's sketch from a dry riverbed

artists approached their work and how dedicated they were. It made for a quiet, peaceful camp. At night, I sat in the smoke of the campfire, because it always guaranteed me a seat and no mosquitoes, and listened as the others chatted about their lives and art.

There was a deep sense of wanting Australia to pull up its socks in regard to acknowledging how the country was founded. I have heard it all before but, even so, it is encouraging, even though talk with fellow artists is cheap. Talking with those who disagree with us is the hard slog. It is only those uncomfortable conversations that can bring change. To both sides.

When we got back to Alice Springs I ran into the Aboriginal artist Maree Clarke and another old brother from the early language foundation days. The conversations we had on the footpath galvanised feelings which had been hovering like metal filings around the attraction of a distant magnet.

Maree's understanding of the colony is as good as anyone's and her views brought the magnet closer and the metal fragments attached themselves neatly to the pole, providing the perspective that had been hovering in my thoughts. The way her mind works has always fascinated me, that breadth of perspective, that inspired art.

Her conversation drew my lens into sharp focus.

So, Here's the Dream

After leaving Maree we walked around the town looking for a meal and a beer. Alice is not scary, but the town has a lot of bored black people on the streets, some of them bored and drunk. Most are kids. It is clear that something has broken.

I sat down to write this part of the book after watching poor old Mallacoota try to run a music festival in blizzard conditions and a power outage in the Easter of 2023. The town just kept plugging away, Plan B followed by Plans C, D, E and F.

There was an Aboriginal presence in the programming and they became the heart of it. Kutcha Edwards, as usual, produced one of the great shows, but his niece, Holly Johnson, wasn't far behind. I've known Holly since she was a girl, so I was moved to see her commitment to culture.

I yarned to some of the Gippsland Aboriginal families and marvelled at their strength, and how it had survived such persistent attack.

Unemployment, ice and alcohol are scourges in our community. Suspicion of government is rife, involvement in available health services is low. Why? Well, you run your country perfectly for 100,000 years and then one day the whole thing is snatched away from you. You get treated like animals, shot and raped, the church tells lies about your culture, the school history lessons advise of your inferiority, people gnash their teeth about whether or not to include you in the constitution. Then see how resilient you are.

Traumas like that do not go away quickly, but how have some families risen above the reverberations of dispossession and others have descended into endless desperation and the poverty that haunts misfortune? Many families have not had an employed person beneath their roof for over three generations. You cannot mount a resistance to dispossession while living under such relentless disadvantage.

So, here's the dream. We point out to the government that of all the millions made from Indigenous food only 1 per cent goes to Aboriginal people. We tell them that we will take over all their Aboriginal employment programs and train our people to reform Australian forests and national parks by thinning and cool burning. We employ thousands and thousands in the forests and, in the agriculture and food industry, we employ thousands more.

Professor Marcia Langton, Associate Provost at Melbourne University, cautions that many of our people aren't work ready and it's true. So many Aboriginal people have no experience with the demands of work and planning for it. It is not beyond us, but it is learnt behaviour, you learn it by watching your parents do it, not from a dopey training program designed only to calm the hearts of decent Australians.

I have seen Aboriginal people trained and trained to do menial tasks by non-Aboriginal people who are simply going through the motions, knowing that there is no job available. On the other hand, I have seen Aboriginal people trained by other Aboriginal people with entirely different results. It works when slackness isn't tolerated. Government programs can't do this because they are toy programs, there is no urgency or real expectation of them being completed or honoured.

On the farm, the jobs have to get done, your brothers and sisters depend on your commitment. In the forest it works the same, it requires a team to make the job safe. If someone is away the job can't be completed and everybody suffers.

For that commitment and skill you get paid, your children have shoes, their teeth are fixed and nobody, nobody can tell you what to do.

I have stood in Centrelink queues with Aboriginal people who have needed support in putting their case. It is demoralising, a waste of time and energy, and the department owns you. Many of the staff are good people but their rules mean they have to treat adults like children and that means people learn to behave like children; always in the naughty corner.

I see a different future. I see us being able to honour our relationship with Mother Earth to improve Australian agriculture and forestry. We can develop a truly Australian cuisine based on the old food production techniques and, instead of stealing it from us, Australia pays us for the produce and, in doing so, we reduce carbon emissions, we preserve scarce water resources and we build soil, because ours are Australian plants, they do not have to be coddled like hot house flowers. These are not platitudes, we actually perform these miracles on the farm, but it's not magic, it's the result of simply treating Australia like herself.

In the dream I see our community buy one of the four bakeries which have closed down in our district over the last few years. We train our kids to be bakers and retailers, then we buy the local pub and turn it into a top-class cafe and restaurant. We train our people to be chefs and waiters, managers, retailers.

We buy the old petrol station which closed a decade ago and turn it into an electric vehicle recharge hub. Then we buy the tour boat and train half a dozen young people to get a Coxswain's certificate (to allow them to operate a boat in sheltered waters) and run bird and history tours around the lakes. Recently we could have bought all of those things for less than a million dollars. I have seen stores of boots and clothing for abandoned training programs worth twice that amount.

What an investment it would be. What a return on the country's investment. What pride and independence for the people. I think we could make massive change to our country very cheaply but Australia will have to let go of its mission complex. Don't contemplate what can be done to fix Aboriginal people but instead begin thinking about how depleted Australian forests and farms can be revived with Aboriginal involvement.

It begins with changing the constitution. I am convinced that when the Australian people recognise Aboriginal people as the first peoples and acknowledge that the country was stolen from a viable society and economy all sorts of justice will flow.

That justice is pent up in the Australian people. You can feel it. Australia wants to take this step but some politicians and journalists cannot let go of the keys to the mission gate.

Those people are hanging on to a roast beef and royal coach idea of Australia and, like the megafauna, seem unaware that they themselves are disappearing. Do not let the dying dinosaur sweep you away with its vengeful tail. Feel sorry for Dino if you wish, but don't let him, yes him, flirt with the worst side of your human nature.

Dino, piss off and hunt sparrows, we're going to look after the Golden Whistler, the lyrebird and dingo; we want to be free, we want to be Australians.

The Currawong Grid and the Whale Pattern

We are now in the depth of winter and the currawongs have settled into a pattern. They are still gathering on the grass to the south of the Illamee garden, spacing themselves evenly and standing stock still before dashing forward a couple of paces and stabbing at something on the ground. This feeding behaviour is so well organised, so neatly geometric.

Meanwhile, Gurandgi are working hard to get our whale ceremony prepared. Marnie is keen to come so we picked her up from the airport and drove on to Narooma in preparation for the following day's ceremony at Nangudga.

At dawn we performed the Grandfather Sun ceremony and then went to the estuary to honour the arrival of the whales. We worked hard at it from 11 am to 5 pm. Family and guests were invited and there were probably thirty-five of us on the beach. It is always such a moving ceremony. As the oldest woman in attendance, Lyn led the women into the circle and I could see how moved she was. The old dancer in her couldn't be suppressed but I knew her knees would be quite remorseful the next day.

Preparing the dance ground

I was thrilled that brother Jacob Cassidy came down all the way from Forrest Beach near Townsville to bring his grandfather's whale story to us. It was a moving thing to hear and meshed seamlessly with ours. It is our ambition to stitch all these stories into the old religious pre-colonial cloak.

I will visit Jacob soon on his Country where he will give me the full story and we will talk to the community about our food journey. Jacob's community are very culturally active and have a venture where they convert old cars to run on electricity. In turn they are interested in our employment creation.

I was emotionally exhausted by the ritual for Gurawul but I had to get on a plane to Parkes to meet up with my brother Stretch. Geoff Anderson is a long streak of duck shit and I have called him Stretch for the twenty years we have worked together on language.

Brother had organised a big few days of language and cultural activities and there were so many young people involved it was really heartening. Stretch showed us the house where he was born and where the divide between black and white in Parkes was enforced right up to the 1980s.

Stretch trawls through Trove and often sends me details about our family and on this trip was able to talk about where part of our family lived. I was so grateful because I knew they had lived somewhere in the district.

The night session in the museum was a moving program, the local families sharing their stories and jokes.

Next day's travel was arduous but when I got home I met Lyn on the track in drizzling rain. We greeted Grandfather the next day in the same fine mist but after ceremony I had to go straight into a series of Zooms and meetings. Kuboka was singing his heart out in the Lucerne tree near the clothesline and an Eastern Spinebill was enjoying the first bottlebrush flowers. Participants on the Zoom could hear the joy of my friends. Country always heals, and their voices were the balm of normality. Home.

We had guests from Yambulla down at the farm and Noel and Trish and the fellas cooked up a chicken and lily curry and baked two beautiful loaves of bread. These moments are very significant in the reclamation of our food culture and having family and community around always makes it special.

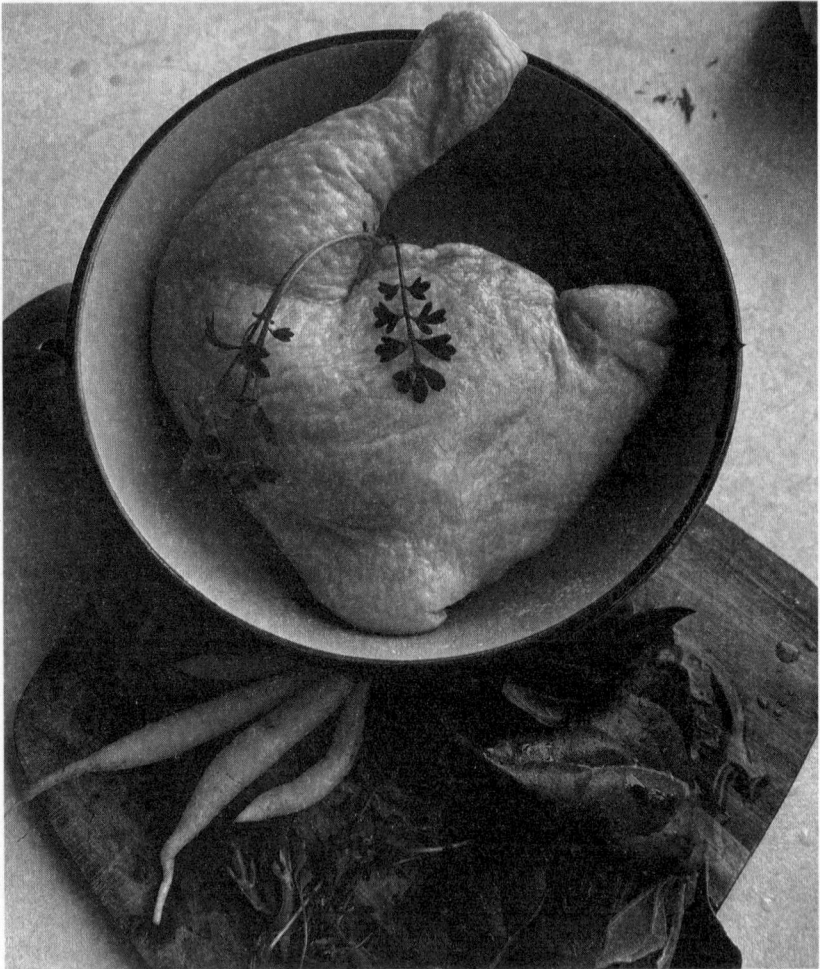

Chicken, lilies and greens

I look forward to the day when Australians think nothing of eating seared lily root and roo curry with Kangaroo Grass bread and Warrigal Green tapenade.

That food culture belongs at the farm. It grows in our ground and is told in our hills. Looking west from the paddocks a flat hill can be seen as a blue blur in between two closer mounts. Yuin man Graham Moore told us that this is the giant damper that two greedy brothers tried to hide in the trees so that they could have it all to themselves. To punish their selfishness, Daramah, the great creator, called up a violent wind which felled the trees and brought the damper down on the brothers, killing them.

Many of our legends are about the sin of greed, but they also remind us that the story of breadmaking is attached to our soil, that we are following a tradition so ancient that it has its own story etched in the land. The Old People prepared their bread and tubers right where we do and the cautionary tale of the greedy brothers peeps at us from the surrounding hills. We are reassured that we are following ancient lore.

Some have said that baking was unknown in southern districts but there are several stories which make it obvious that breads were made all over Australia. The greedy brothers' story is told in many locations and we are glad to have our local version of the tale but, more importantly, it is a daily reminder, as we look up from the labour in the paddocks, that bread is part of our culture.

We are aware of ancient food provision on the farm when we turn up stone tools. Terry found a wonderful little edge ground axe right at the site of our new shed. That small tool is our talisman and protector.

Meanwhile, we are still working on the filming for *The Dark Emu Story*. That bloody bird won't leave me alone. Allan Clarke arrived from Blackfella Films so that we could work through the script. It is pleasant work because Allan is such a good bloke, but tiring,

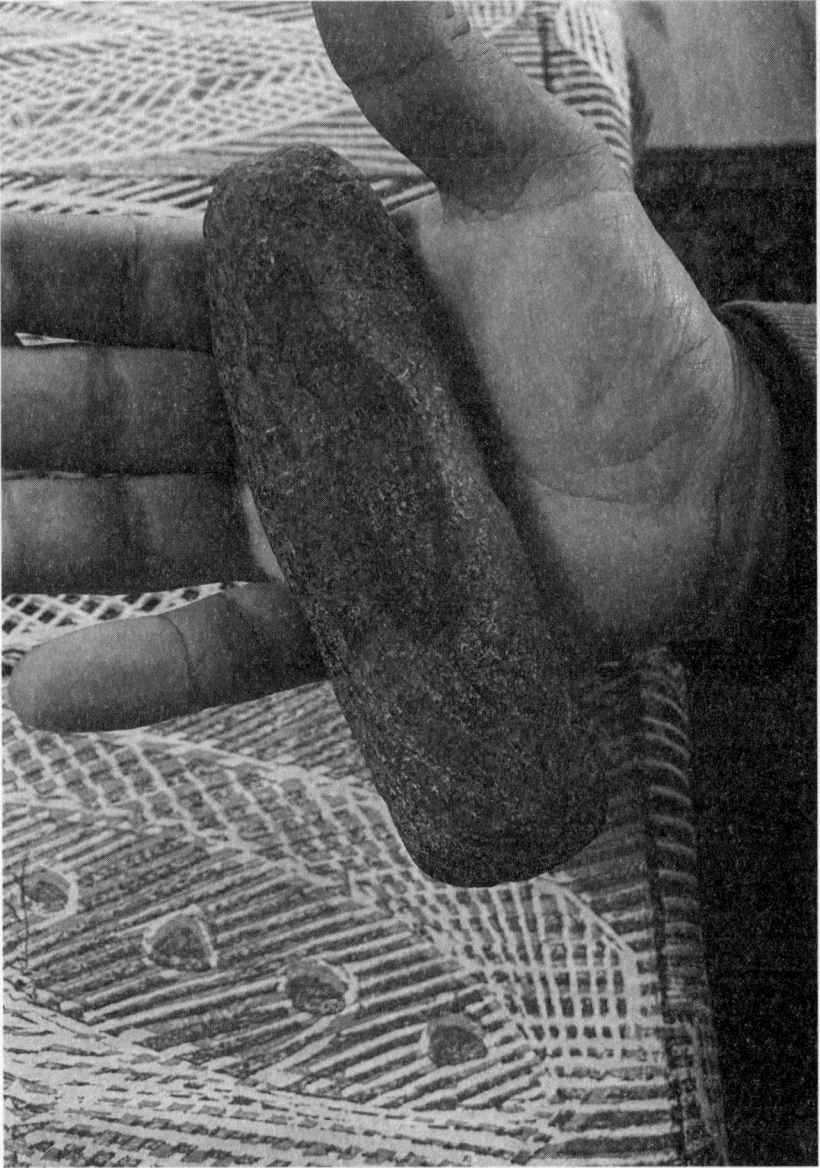

Ground axe excavated near our new shed site

nonetheless. I'm aware that I often complain about tiredness, but it is a fact of my life these days.

Neither am I as tolerant of cold weather. There was a severe frost on the last day of July and it made me ache.

I pruned the grapevine and sprayed the fruit trees for curly leaf and later worked on the compost bins.

Lyn and I went for dinner at the Sea Horse Inn, one of those sanctuaries of mine during the fires and Covid lockdowns. I don't know how they stayed open but they did. Those respites are legendary oases in my mind. On this night there was a clear sky with a wonderful sunset and small waves sighing onto the beach.

Early Spring

It is the season of eggs and babies so there is vibrant energy and anxiety everywhere. Snakes and goannas appear, orchids bloom, the bream are breeding in the deep holes upriver.

Birran Durran Durran Brings the Spring

The Spur-winged Plovers are very active. They strut about in a very upright posture while the currawongs take up their stations on the grass again. Those birds still steal the soap from the outside shower and nip more buds off the apple tree but they are family and have to be tolerated. As Uncle Max said, Patience, Tolerance, Respect.

The bowerbirds too are on the grass in front of the house and appear to be eating seed. I think they are targeting Flickweed. The Eastern Spinebill is slipping through the wire mesh to visit the bottle-brush tree in the Nullama garden while the Yellow-rumped Thornbill visits the bottlebrush near the kitchen window. It is as regular as clockwork at the beginning of spring. I know there is supposed to be another month before spring begins but the birds have called it, they are thinking about the excitement of eggs.

The plovers were running beside each other with their heads slightly down this afternoon and Koon ar rook (Wood Ducks), are running at each other with their necks outstretched. There's an air of vibrance pulsating on the farm.

The young male Buru are still boxing each other enthusiastically and I never tire of watching them as I shower in the morning.

Terry, Nathan and I went out into the bush to cut some big coolamon blanks so that we can prepare some for the cultural camps that we hope will be coming up in March. When we first began our lore camps fifteen years ago there was a lot of plastic food packaging and utensils but, gradually, we are replacing the buckets and bowls with handmade objects. Our preparatory activities are contributing to the sense of anticipation.

As we finish up, Jitti Jitti (Willy Wagtail) is calling incessantly as the sun sets and the male Buru are scratching the tails of the females with great concentration. Frogs are calling loudly and swallows are hawking. The mood is intense and during the day we looked up from our work to comment on the activity.

The fellas made a beautiful coolamon and a paint pot out of the timber we gathered today and we're looking forward to using them on our camp. These objects become familiar to Gurandgi with repeated use and we proudly tell new arrivals of the provenance of each.

I did a lot of tractor work the following day and, while the clutch pedal plays gyp with my knees, there was a beautiful fingernail moon in the north west to salve my pain.

Next morning, while I was in the shower, two young deer ran down the track and past the Water Ribbon Dam and continued all the way to the Phoenix shed where they disappeared from sight.

Wonga Pigeons called incessantly all day, joining the excitement of the season.

I had to leave early next morning and fly to Adelaide and then on to Wilpena Pound to be part of Warndu's cultural festival. It is hard to resist invitations from community even when we are busy with our own work.

Damien Coulthard took me to some petroglyph and art sites in the gorge. Isaiah, Kristian Coulthard and Pauline McKenzie told me the stories of their Country including the two snakes that formed Wilpena Pound. These two snakes are huge players in Yuin story too.

The young Dieri people asked about our culture camps and I explained how one man's determination to save his culture created a movement which saw seventy-five men at the last lore camp. In all, there are more than 150 Gurandgi, not always singing from the same song sheet, but all committed to cultural revival. I encouraged them to understand that they were capable of doing the same. They had the stories, they just had to enlist the enthusiasm of their cousins. Easier said than done, but what is the alternative?

Flinders Ranges, Wilpena Pound

I returned home and even though it was freezing cold I couldn't be bothered lighting the fire. The currawongs were calling chewy chowa, a really distinctive call which I only hear at that time of year.

I went into the bush and cut some bends for boomerangs so that we can take them to our next lore camp. They become precious when we make them ourselves, from material off Country, but the great joy is seeing them get used by the brothers. A set of boomerangs clapped in ceremony, an ochre pot being used during preparation, a coolamon full of Bura (fish) and Walkun (abalone); it really imbues the object with memory and spirit.

I love hearing young fellas tell new Gurandgi about these things, it convinces me the culture isn't dead.

Goomera, the Possum

Mount Ellery used to be known as Mount Goongerah or Goomera. It is a peak near the town of Goongerah and Uncle Max told me I had to climb it and find its story and tell it to other Gurandgi.

Lyn and I had climbed the mountain with another Aboriginal man, Clayton Harrison, decades ago, and he showed us the giant boulders which were the eggs of the Rainbow Serpent. Uncle Max knew about them but there were other things we needed to look out for.

We made repeated attempts to climb the mountain but all sorts of things intervened. The fires stopped us in 2019, then Covid and other people's health.

Mount Ellery, Goongerah

I climbed it with Lyn and Wayne Thorpe in 2022 but Wayne's health condition prevented him from getting to the summit and Lyn's knees limited her.

It was a wild day and the dead spars of trees killed by the fires were clashing like the spears of warriors and deadly shafts were raining down around me, but I got up there and took some photos. Uncle Max was pleased that I had recognised some elements of the story but there was still something else we needed to observe.

Lyn and I and Terry made another attempt on 11 August. We tried coming from the east but it was too rough so we went back to the western side and climbed again. Terry and I got to the top but once again the spears were clashing. We were about to inspect the north-east side when a huge ink black cloud loomed in from the west and we scuttled back down the track, picking up Lyn as we went and just got back before the storm smashed onto the top of the car.

Next time Terry and I are going to camp at the base and climb in the still of the dawn. Once we have seen the story Uncle left for me in code there are several other mountains we have to climb, chapters of a bigger story.

Part of Uncle's aim was to record how much of the coast can be seen from each peak. It was only a small element of the task but it was to be part of his plan to recreate the trail of smoke old Aboriginal people sent up as they communicated the progress of Captain Cook's Endeavour sailing up the east coast in 1770.

We were well into that plan when the 2019 bushfires put a stop to it. We began again after the fires but then Uncle 'left his suitcase behind' and began a journey in the afterworld. Soon we will begin that project again so that Australia can experience the Invasion from our point of view, share the moment in history from both sides. Healing.

Yellow-faced Honeyeater

The Yellow-faced Honeyeater had been calling for a fortnight in the forest on the north boundary. It is a bold, insistent call and I always associate it with summer. Those months were not with us yet but one honeyeater was laying the platform for his summer lore.

The plovers and Mudlarks had also become very antsy; it was that time of year. The Wonga too was in full voice and that morning I saw two swallows mating after which the female gave a call. I pay a lot of attention to what Giyong Budjarn (Welcome Swallow) has to say, but I'd never heard this song before. It stayed with me all day.

Yellow-faced Honeyeater (Leonie Daws)

The Jacky Winter's song changed from its winter call of peter, peter, peter to a more complex lyric. The whole district was preparing itself for the fecundity of spring.

I went for a long walk in freezing conditions to where I knew Mick was building a track for the son of News Corp's New York director. After a decade of being hammered by that climate denying, Trump loving, black hating scandal rag they move in next door. What are the chances? I feel as if the river has been defiled. It is so wild and remote we thought we were free from the rich, but no, they have their tentacles everywhere; Jungaa (the octopus).

The cold gets into my bones more easily these days and I was morose as I trudged back through the sodden bush.

I got a call from Chris and Terry who were up at Narrabri, north-central New South Wales, showing the local mob how to use the harvester on their grain crops. We get on really well with Kerrie Saunders but there are some white academics working there who are scathing and insulting about Aboriginal knowledge and sovereignty.

Chris was upset by the insults but it happens to us all the time. Some white people get a sniff of Aboriginal culture and knowledge and overnight they become the experts, and not long after that, the owner. We have to guard against it all the time. But the personal attacks still sting.

I lightly roasted some Munyang for tea, so sweet and crunchy. The sugars caramelised on the outside of the tuber, candying their sweetness. It was such a mild and lovely evening and the Garramagang (magpies) and currawongs were noisy right through the night.

The next morning three galahs flew into the Lucerne tree and began cracking seeds. The seeds were still green and I wondered how they digest them. They didn't feed long so perhaps they had to get some drier roughage to help their crop break the seeds down.

As I made an extra nesting box for the ducks, I could hear the Yellow-faced Honeyeater again and the very thought of warmer weather being beckoned cheered me up.

The ducks have a favourite nesting box and squabble over it so I tried to make something similar to ease community tensions.

Nathan saw two golden dingoes on the northern boundary. The kangaroos are nervous but I love the fact that these wild canines still exist here.

One curious duck

Nikeysha Lansborough came to work today to see how she liked it. She's a good young kid but school doesn't appeal to her so we hope she can settle into the farm work. Nikeysha's family are the Mongtas with strong Ngarigo connections to coast and mountains.

Lyn and I travelled to Apollo Bay to see Jack, Shell and Lily. I played Ravel's *Boléro* on the way and was, once again, entranced by its form. It takes over the soundtrack of my life and colours everything it touches, everything moves to the insistence of its rhythm. I have heard people say it is boring and repetitive but perhaps they haven't been watching Country while they listened.

We loved seeing Jack and Shell and having Lily show us her 'school' and everything in her yard. Wangarabell and I reclined on a couch with Lily and read stories. Wangarabell hardly woke but she was good company.

Jack and I did a cultural burn on the block of land we have at Cape Otway. It is wild country but we were able to burn so safely that Lily would leave her game of buried treasure and walk up to us at the edge of the flames and report on her progress.

This is what our burns should be, calm, peaceful activities with the sounds of children's voices and laughter and the amiable snuffling of dogs.

When the CFA fights we put on uniforms; it is as if we are going to war. The vehicles are set up with sirens and disaster survival protection. All of it necessary for the danger of modern fire, but the ancient fire is safe and comfortable and is complemented by children and dogs and chicken sandwiches.

Australia seems ready to embrace this style of care but it is expensive because it requires a series of cool fires in winter managed by squads of Blackfellas and their children. Can the exchequer get its head around the economy of safe fire? One of my neighbours has

Jack and Lily walking with fire

begun burning in this way too and it makes us all safer and the bush more like the old, open park-like Aboriginal forest.

Does Australia want to pay fire soldiers with all their gadgetry or Blackfellas in summer shirts working in the bush every possible day? Let's get the accountants on to it, because I bet our way is cheaper and you don't have Ash Wednesdays and Black Saturdays. It will take decades of hard work but will create a safer and more productive Australia. The grass we make flour from grows in response to gentle fire. We will be able to eat our new safety.

The morning after I got back to Yumburra from Apollo Bay the air was a cacophony of Garramagang, currawongs, bowerbirds and Mudlarks. On the drive home I did three Zooms about language, food and the environment and this morning I did another two, but the reason for them is that so many Australians are on the brink of changing their mind about how to live on this continent. Black people must support them. White people must honour our trust.

One of my old school students is a plumber, Les Bruce. He came out all this way to fix a problem with the solar hot water service. I introduced him to the fellas who were processing seed in the old Cream Shed.

Les was impressed and I thought how important it is for Australians to learn about this way of caring for Country. Les is from one of Mallacoota's old fishing families, many of whom have interesting relations, and I doubt that Les and I vote for the same people, but he is a generous soul and there is no reason for us not to agree on most things, like decency and hard work. I try to keep up my side of the hard work but sometimes I get weary and jaded.

The currawongs and bowerbirds were still feeding on the grass in their spatially separated matrix. I watched them closely to try and understand the scheme. The farm is often a lonely place so these creatures are my friends.

My sombre mood lends itself to the music of Satie and Brenda Gifford as I worked on the star book. The weather was still cool but the Lucerne tree was looking magnificent with a cloak of white flowers. As I went into Genoa to pick up my mail I saw a lovely golden dingo near the bridge in Maree's paddock.

I flew to Byron Bay for the writers festival and got there late and sat in the tropical garden trying to understand how to order food by QR code. Whatever happened to English?

A young waiter must have looked at my clothes and boots and thought, yokel, and brought me a beer unbidden. It was the act of an angel. The only thing I could order at that hour was chicken wings but they were delicious.

The festival is a favourite of mine. I should be philosophically opposed to the hyper-hip Byron but it's too beguiling. Blackfella writer mates are always there and we yarn and have a drink and a bit of food and just laugh, laugh, laugh. Such a relief.

Julie Clark arrived after getting back from visiting her daughter and grandson in Fiji. Julie is a very close friend and one of the minds I turn to when I need an intelligent answer. She came back to sort out the papers of her late husband, Richard Neville, but then went to a party in the hills full of very wealthy and famous people so that I could interview a man about a massacre of Aboriginal people on one of the beaches in North Queensland during World War II.

It is his mother's story and I have been chasing it for a few years now but it is always just out of reach. The mother is ill or she's about to record her memories or the son is too busy to dig out the pile of documents.

A massacre of Aboriginal people seems to be hovering on the edge of Australia's consciousness while a family fiddles about in the attic. I find it so upsetting that such a significant event is being treated so casually.

Julie has such a great mind. Her company is so important to me. She has a wry intelligence, as sharp as the edge of a ground pipi shell, but it is interrupted by exquisite jokes. And she knows everyone. We had a drink in the bar and Bryan Brown said hullo, Rachel Ward yarned for hours, everyone who is anyone loves Julie. It is entrancing watching this incredibly modest woman negotiate the richest and most famous. And she knows books and writing so deeply. It was no accident that she was an editor in New York. This is such a foreign world to me but I am swept up by the talk and opinions.

Young Corey Tutt rocked up too. Corey wrote *The First Scientists*. He has a brilliant mind but talks at a million miles an hour. I love the fact that these young Blackfellas are appearing at literary festivals and providing Aboriginal knowledge for readers.

On the way home I had a really good yarn with Van Badham, another of Julie's friends. She has made an incredibly brave stance on exposing the corruption of the internet. I understood what her position had cost her and was full of admiration.

Festivals are rich in conversation and I always love them but I caught the flu.

I tried to organise a tortuous travel schedule for the following week as well as write changes for my play, *Cutter and Coota*. The First Languages Australia board are also very busy with new staff appointments.

Gurandgi Dean Kelly's father had died and we're trying to support Cooma's film *Where the Water Starts* as well as contribute to his land restoration work. Part of the responsibility of Gurandgi is to support the work of our brothers. It's the lore.

I became very ill and had to take to my bed to read manuscripts sent by young black writers. Their work is such an inspiration but I'm struggling to concentrate.

Bunjil, the Wedge-tailed Eagle, was wheeling about and Galoo, the White-faced Herons, were cruising about in their languid flap and drift courting dance. Giyong Budjarn, the Welcome Swallow, was nesting and I saw one fly about with a white feather which it kept dropping and retrieving. If it's a signal or advertisement it is very eye-catching.

I did a Covid test, negative, but had to sleep for a bit as I felt so doggy. Dale Winward's school group came over from his farm to learn about Murnong and Munyang, so I had to get up. Fortunately, they were keen weeders and will be back the next day. Chris and Terry will cook them a loaf of bread made from our flour.

I learnt that some Aboriginal people are closing down any discussion of the Wurdi Youang site near the You Yangs. I know that community have to keep some elements of their culture to themselves but this site is of world importance as it shows an ancient relationship with celestial knowledge. I had always hoped it would help Australians better understand the culture they had dispossessed. There is so much to do, so many sensitivities to negotiate.

Lyn's painting of the Moon Rise

The moon rose in the west and in the morning, 1 September, I heard the first Black-faced Cuckoo-shrike of the season. The wing shuffler is a favourite bird of mine and it made me realise that this book should be the story of birds, fish and animals. While Dale's Steiner school kids were around, I saw the Nankeen Kestrel land in the big dead tree in front of the house. As Uncle always reminded us, nothing is ever really dead and this old, leafless tree is a focus of so much life.

I gave each of the kids one of my adolescent novels and the school-teacher with them told me that my collection of stories, *Salt*, was the last book her father had read before he died.

I thought of that man's bedside book as I counted thirty kangaroos grazing on the flat near the Cumbungi Dam. The Koon ar rook (Wood Ducks) were pairing off and feeding together. The male walked behind her and didn't eat much himself but looked about, forever vigilant, while she plumped up.

The trip to Sydney was plagued by travel chaos but I finally got to speak to the university students who had been studying the *Cutter and Coota* play. After that session I tried to fly back home but the flight was cancelled and I had to haul my bags down to the good old Mantra Hotel feeling pretty crook.

When I got back home, completely wrecked, I did a Covid test: positive. I rang Lyn and she brought over some soup but I was too sick to eat any.

In the last few months several neighbours had died and I missed them. You can see the way my thoughts were drifting. Maree Brackley down at the bridge. Barbara Triggs out at Dead Finish and

Dawn Joiner at Redbanks. With so much of the past disappearing I felt lonely and maudlin.

I stayed in bed all the next day and kept hearing tap tap tap at the window. I thought it was the Mudlarks clipping spiders off the glass but they were in fact looking in the mirror of the verandah glass and fighting off the very handsome male on the other side.

I forced myself to go for a walk and found a host of Nodding Greenhoods up near Bun Bun Gungwan. As I was walking back home I thought I saw Paul Davis's boat going upstream, a distinctive blue plastic vessel. Paul passed away suddenly a couple of months ago, so to see his boat triggered my memories of such a young father dying. I taught with his mum decades ago at Mallacoota. It is hard not to be affected by local deaths.

Lyn tested positive too and took to her bed. The online nurses were fantastic. People whinge about public health but I think the state looks after us very well and that is why I have always loved paying tax. I don't understand why people resent paying for their mother's hospitalisation and their children's schooling.

I went by boat to Lyn's to help her with dinner but she was much better than me, having caught her infection early and therefore able to receive the benefit of the anti-virals.

I was working on language Zooms at the farm over a couple of days but after the last one finished I went straight to bed, not being able to look at food or even a beer. And, as my family know, that is a sign I am close to death!

Good old Mick was back to grading the track. I could hear his machines grinding away down near the Water Ribbon dam and every now and then I checked his progress from my bed. Geez, I was crook.

The Queen died last night. Bloody hell, everyone is falling off the perch.

I drove up to the Snowy Mountains because Cooma was taking us on a cultural tour of sites we have to see so that he can give us part of their story.

Lyn was battling the Emergency Services Victoria bureaucrats to sway them to the view of burning more regularly and with less intensity. They all nod their heads pleasantly, but do nothing.

Lightning and Thunder

From Cooma, the Gurandgi drove west to view the valley systems from a lookout on a bluff. The Snowy River starts near the Pinch and we followed it downstream to a point where we could cross it in a raft. We were there to investigate the Emu, Lyrebird and Eagle story.

As soon as we set foot on the other side, three Gungwan (emus) came down to inspect us. They stayed with us for some time before moving on and we took this as a welcome and followed a series of scar and modified trees through the site. This Country was badly burnt during the fires and some significant trees have been lost but it remains really powerful Country, marked by the spiritual intensity of the people.

Cooma took us back across the river and we climbed out of the valley to a site between the Bobundara River and Dalgety where two conflicting brothers were punished for their selfish and needless fighting.

Mirribi was turned into a hill comprising red ochre and Malaba into a white hill as Dharama, the great creator, became frustrated by the brother's continuous and wasteful bickering. He urged them not to waste their energies but rather contribute that energy to the community, but like many men they persisted in their useless enmity.

The fighting resulted in Malaba losing a leg and the recovery from his injury marks the landscape. Mirribi was still jealous of his more athletic brother, who despite his injury could still dance. This infuriated Mirribi and he tried to go one better in the disability stakes but didn't have the fortitude. Dharama was thoroughly tired of their selfishness and stepped in to turn them into rather nondescript hills.

You can see that I have had to prune the detail for cultural reasons but for Gurandgi standing on that freezing windswept plain it was a lesson that had relevance and impact. Male ego. It has to be restrained, it has to be creative, it has to be directed to the good of community.

Sometimes the best energies of humans are used to fuel foolish disputes. Wars in Sudan and Ukraine are fueled by many things but the contest between male egos seems to be uppermost.

We stood on the plain as the wind whistled around us. That story and its relevance to all men today was given to Cooma by a man who was raised by his grandmother, Granny Tongiai, a woman who was born around the time of the first entry of white people into her country.

Granny was the keeper of the magical beetles, another story about which I have to be circumspect, but let's just say that Granny was a soothsayer. To have her stories relayed to us by impeccable authority is a great blessing for the lore of the land. That group of men standing beside the road in the glacial wind were as solid a group of men as you will find, but Dharama's message cautioned us to consider the difficulties we had encountered since Uncle Max's passing. Those divisions happened, but to what purpose, and at what expenditure of energy? We survived the rancour because of dedication to the instructions left to us. That diplomacy has to be protected and sheltered by grace.

Cooma brought us to that plain to help us understand where we had been and why we must hold the lore sacred above all else.

I left my brothers as they prepared to drive north and I drove south toward southern Yuin land. I watched in my mirror as they huddled together digesting the lore of the land. I can't remember too many more important moments in my life.

I had plenty of time to think about it as I drove on the lonely road to Bobundara and Bombala. There was an iron frost descending on the alps and the window lights of the very occasional house spoke of a welcome domesticity, the weak flicker of life.

The brothers' story haunted me all of the next day but Lyn wanted to investigate a section of the Genoa Creek Track where we might recommend some mosaic burning to reluctant local authorities. Nudging them toward a consensus on cool burns is time consuming and largely unprofitable but that is no excuse to stop trying. This is our Country we are defending.

When I got back to the farm I found more Nodding Greenhoods and Caladenia catanata up near the tiny houses. The season has changed.

As proof of that change Birran Durran Durran now has chicks. We tried to count them but the plovers were refusing close inspection.

Next morning the currawongs were calling look where, look where, with an upward inflection at the end. They have various calls and one of them is Baracello, Baracello. I have never known as many in the valley at once and I hope they are not predating the plover chicks as well as my soap.

They have a particular flight pattern for long swoops over the valley. They flick their wings and glide in slow loops before switching their wings again like a desultory boy playing slowly with a flick knife.

As Yedding (Moon) rose in the east we listened to the frogs' great and insistent orchestra. Using the FrogID app Lyn estimated that we were hearing Common Eastern Froglet, Brown Tree Frog, Whistling Tree Frog and Peron's Tree Frog. I like to be able to distinguish one

Twin Nodding Greenhoods: Pterostylis nutans

bird from another, one frog from another, they are so miraculous they deserve the dignity of a name.

I was about to sit down for a cup of tea when I noticed a Mudlark lying on its back on the other side of the glass screen that protects the language table on the verandah. As I put my cup down to inspect the bird I disturbed a Collared Sparrowhawk that must have been trying to get to the dead bird. It swooped away and gave me a good old fright. I wondered how long the hawk had been studying the Mudlark, confused as to why it couldn't get to it. Had the hawk stooped on the lark and killed it or surprised it midflight so that the Mudlark veered away in panic and into the glass?

The sparrowhawk is such a shy and wild animal it was a privilege to see up close the flare of its marbled wings. I tossed the old lark out on to the lawn so that someone could make use of it.

I think that poor bird was the one who had been tapping away at the glass trying to fend off a rival. Well, both were dead now but, as Uncle Max would have said, nothing is really dead. The lark would fuel another life.

I had a busy afternoon planting my spring vegetables; tomatoes, cucumbers, pumpkins and chillies. I love the Old People's vegetables but old habits die hard, the food of my childhood impossible to resist. I was about to get to that cup of tea at last when Clive Blazey of Diggers nursery turned up wanting to talk about bushfires. Just as Clive left, a German environmental student arrived to talk about sustainability. I boiled the kettle again and was about to sit down when Billy Mack, Aboriginal actor, rang to mourn the death of the great Jack Charles.

The following morning was cold and frosty but, typically, was followed by a glorious day. A galah got itself caught behind the glass screen on the verandah. Is it something to do with the light at this time of year? As I approached the bird to help it out, two other galahs sat on the verandah rail and screamed and screamed at me. They performed a violent display of flashing out their wings full stretch.

The trapped galah freed itself but I wondered if the shrieking was to praise me for my assistance or admonish me for laying a fiendish trap.

Galahs are such interesting birds. If there is a summer shower they will perform high wire gymnastics on the power lines, hanging upside down and screeching, complete circus idiots. I have seen them competing to stand on lemons in the front yard of our bed and breakfast Riverbend, to see who can stand the longest while the fruit rolls beneath them. Tell me that birds don't play! But what is the purpose of such antics?

Fly West, Drive North

Lyn and I flew west for the Quantum Words festival in Perth, but Lyn became sick straight away. I did a big gig with other writers to 300 school students and then other events in a crowded schedule.

It was a lovely hotel but Lyn was crook as a dog. We met up with Noel and Trish who were touring the west as part of their fire healing. We had a few beers in a chaotic restaurant on the waterfront where some public holiday was in full swing.

A lot of my work was in and around the museum so we could go anywhere we liked. I was a child again, peering into glass cases, trying to get the animated displays to work.

I fell in love with some replica planets at the bookshop. They are powered by magnets and appear to revolve in space. I literally watched one for half an hour. I bought one for my son-in-law who, I hoped, would appreciate the scientific artistry.

Years ago, I was at the Margaret River Reader and Writers Festival and an old Nyoongar bloke drove up from Albany to tell me a story. He wasn't at all interested in the festival but insisted on talking to me about whales. He took us down to where the river ran into the ocean and his son sang and danced the story of how the whale left the land and became an ocean mammal. It is one of the great stories of the world and meshes so closely with our Yuin whale story. I will never forget stepping out of the car and having the hair creep on the back of my neck. I felt like I knew exactly what the young man, Zac, would sing, and I was right because I recognised some of the words in his song as Yuin.

Not only were they singing a similar song to ours, they were using some of the same language. Did that song come from the east to the west or west to east? Whichever way it travelled it showed the strength of Aboriginal connection across the continent. It was one of the great moments of my life and, as a result, the family who shared the story are never far from my thoughts.

I rang Uncle Max and told him of what I had seen and heard and he was quiet. I waited. 'So,' he said at last, 'what do you think?' 'I think you should see it for yourself, make sure I've got it right.'

He agreed and we made the preparations to meet the Webbs on their Country near Margaret River. Just as the father and son began to tell, sing and dance the whale story, I was overcome with a wave of horror. What if the old man thinks this is nonsense? I forgot to breathe until I realised it was hurting, but right then I saw the old man smile and cast me a glance of affirmation.

What a relief. If I had dragged the old man all that way for something he thought had no consequence I would be guilty of several lore crimes. But as the whale's western story was revealed, Uncle began to shuffle in time with the dance and I knew that my instinct was correct; all these old stories are connected.

While we were there, Uncle and I travelled to Albany, Perth and Broome discussing the linkages of whale stories. So much was revealed but there is much more to come. The story is so important to all Aboriginal and Torres Strait Islander people because it binds us together, parts of the one story. The story can bind Australians too and I am planning to visit a dozen communities where I have been invited to listen to elements of the great story encompassing us all.

It was years since I had seen Wayne and Toni Webb, old friends who introduced me to their people's whale story a decade ago, so while I was in Perth I arranged to meet them at Margaret River. Lyn was still too sick to travel so I met them at their new place. They told me a tale of woe about being dudded in business and it sounded so much like our recent experience. They were reduced to living in a little old house thanks to the kindness of a white person they had worked with for decades.

Wayne has been a warrior for his people all his life so I found this story deeply depressing. But the fire in Wayne was undimmed and it made me wish he could have met Noel Butler. They would have recognised the culture man within each other; and the pain they had each endured.

I got Lyn to see a doctor because she was getting no better and we had to fly home the next day. It was a long flight and Lyn suffered whereas I love those flights because I get three hours of uninterrupted work. Nevertheless, we were both feeling pretty wrecked by the time we got to Sydney.

Lyn flew on to the south coast and I flew to Coffs Harbour and hired a four-wheel drive so I could work at a festival with Gurandgi brothers Jeremy and Barry. I stayed overnight on the way to Murwillumbah and the only place I could get was the pub at Coramba. Interesting. But comfortable. I had a countery at the bar and a couple of schooners while the locals raffled chooks for the sports club. Of course, I practised my trade by listening to the conversations around me and absorbed the stories revealed by clothing styles and the fingers frittering beer coasters or turning wine glasses in tight circles.

I love nights like that. I am the stranger, just some anonymous old dude at the bar, but I am surrounded by story and because I know none of them it can find its way into my fiction. I remember whole slabs of dialogue from those human intimacies.

I retreated to the accommodation warren and was able to wash and dry some clothes. The place was full of voices but no bodies. Food was cooked in the kitchen and instant coffee drunk but I saw no one. Pub of ghosts.

It rained all day and got heavier overnight. Roads went under across the district and the track I took out of that Country had to be deeply convoluted. It took its toll and I had to sleep in the car. I got to the festival in Murwillumbah eventually and did my gigs and yarned up with the Gurandgi brothers including Dakota, a serious young Gurandgi man and poet.

I also met up with my sister Melissa Lucashenko and her brother, John, whom I had been working with on his biography. There were loads of Blackfellas everywhere and the yarns were long but I was about to head off on my biggest adventure so I had to haul myself away so that I could get within striking distance of Windorah.

I watched the AFL Grand Final in some big beer barn at Toowoomba where no one else had the slightest interest in the game. It was luxury. I had a huge screen to myself and had to talk to no one. I slept in the car that night somewhere near Dalby.

I got up early and drove and drove through several different geographic zones and rolled in to Windorah just on dusk.

Australia's First Miners

I had been dreaming of this trip since 2018. Fires, Covid and floods all conspired to thwart every effort to get there until now. Queensland University archaeologist Michael Westaway read *Dark Emu* and wanted to test the hypothesis that Aboriginal people led semi-sedentary lives and engaged in economic and agricultural activity.

A few academics and right-wing journalists were scoffing at these ideas. And not just scoffing, but attempting to eviscerate the very idea of Aboriginal accomplishment.

When the controversy erupted I was bemused because the facts speak for themselves and the outrage seemed to be confected. I think when people look back on this period they will wonder what all the fuss was about. It seems to have more to do with academic pride than scholarship.

European terms like 'farming' cannot accurately describe Aboriginal food propagation methods but hunting and gathering is even further from the truth. It seemed that some in the press were desperate to deflect the idea of economic and agricultural activity in order to maintain the myth of peaceful and justified invasion. The rest of Australia seems ready to accept the obvious.

Mithaka Country is between Windorah and Birdsville in the south-west corner of Queensland. Early colonisers called it the Corner Country because of its location at the junctions of New South Wales, Queensland, the Northern Territory and South Australia. Michael was working with local man Josh Gorringe, on a site where established houses were common and intense systems of trade seemed to have been conducted.

Michael Westaway gathered together a team to investigate, not just the raw archaeological material but also the sedentism those things were suggesting. What did people eat, how did they live, with whom did they trade?

The results reported widely in the media showed that the Mithaka had mined the area intensively for grinding stones. Three million stones had been removed from the site and the vast bulk of those had been traded. Not only were the Mithaka grinding grain crops into flour but many thousands of others were doing it too. The study now hopes to find out how far the Mithaka stones were traded and over how many years.

Grinding stones wear out so groups of people would need replacement stones. But how frequently? We don't know the answer to that yet. Which is why I was so keen to see the sites for myself.

It was an emotional day for me to see the houses. There were many of them, and so beautifully made some still stand today, but seeing the scale of the grinding dish mines was a shock. I was expecting two or three mines but they were everywhere and we still don't know how many there are or over what area. One scientist estimated that 3 million stones had been mined and dressed from these mines alone.

Mithaka house site

It seems the Old People were mining a reef of suitable stone that expressed itself at the surface frequently over a vast area. When I was there the archaeologists were examining a group of mines but, by wandering away from the site by a mere kilometre, I came across a building feature for which we could find no explanation. I imagine that every time the researchers go there they find something new. People will learn a lot about this Australia in the coming decades long after the federal Opposition decided to vote against the proposition that Aboriginal people should be recognised as the First People of the continent. It makes you cringe with embarrassment at the petty malice of this view.

Many people are shortsighted but few deliberately blind themselves. I was reminded of this recalcitrant nastiness when we posted online about our harvests of Aboriginal foods at Black Duck. These foods will have an enormous impact on Australian farming and diet but the trolls wanted to question the extent of my Aboriginality. I find it so depressing that the level of debate about the old Aboriginal society descends so often into churlish contempt.

This story is huge, the world is beginning to know it, but some Australians seem frantic to prove the Invasion did no harm, simply dispossessed a lazy and unproductive people. Three million stones! Lazy?

For me this journey was to honour, not just that story, but an old man and a country for whom I have so much respect. I had been to Birdsville in 2018 and Don Rowlands and I found a site which showed intricate settlements and linked to other similar 'towns' by art.

We had the advantage of travelling in an ABC helicopter while we filmed the documentary, *The Dark Emu Story*, and Don had taken me to the site where he had buried his grandmother. That little oasis is etched in my mind as a paradise, but Don wanted to show me some of the old dome houses and places where others had been before they were burnt down in recent years by pastoralists, or as a lawyer would say, those known to pastoralists.

The trip was so long and convoluted that we had to cross a piece of Country unfamiliar to Don. Suddenly we found ourselves looking at a complex of architectural shapes for which we had no explanation. It was almost dark and fuel was low but we were determined to come back and investigate properly. But life intervened. Fire. Disease. Flood. So, here we are in 2022 and we are packing the ute to visit this site which, for us, has huge significance.

On the way out there, Don was telling me a huge story of two boys and all the while I was thinking of the two brothers in the Australian Alps. And the seventh sister and her Platypus Baby. But that's another story. In fact, it's another book.

We walked across the site and it was shocking to see how intact it was. I have never seen so many tool workshops. I have never seen so much construction. The stone building is breathtaking. We visited two sites but standing on a ridge we could see another four, and just in this valley alone.

We had our lunch in the shade of a Coolabah tree and afterwards Don went to muse in the structures of his old family and his wife, Lyn, and I picked our way through the sites, trying to understand the scale and complexity of the society which had built them.

Lyn called me over to look at something she had found. Someone had arranged stones in a design no bigger than a hearth mat. I looked at her for understanding. 'Someone has drawn the village,' she said.

We looked down at the design in awe. There was the shape of the structures we had walked around and there was the art that linked them to the neighbouring structures 3 kilometres away.

Who would go to that trouble? An older person instructing the young or a young person playing house? It was an extraordinary thing to see and its fragility makes your skin creep. It could be destroyed by a kid on a motorbike. And we could see the tracks of a dirt bike driven by some station worker looking for stock. If he had driven 80 metres to his right he would have masked that story forever.

Andy's gone with cattle and he don't know where he are.

Which is why Don can't countenance archaeologists visiting this site just yet. He wants his own young people to learn it first, to know it, to remember it, to protect it. It's certainly related to all the other archaeology I had visited in the previous days, but there's a probability these sites cross the borders of three states and a territory. It is vast. It is Australia's to know and contemplate, but first it is for Don and his people to explain for us and in that explanation to declare a plan of protection and honour.

I left Don and drove through the gathering darkness to Windorah to catch up with the archaeologists. I wouldn't mention the new site to them because it wasn't my business to do so.

There were three house lights on the whole journey of five hours. I will never forget the journey. I had to concentrate so hard to avoid cattle musing quietly in the middle of the road and all the time I was trying to understand what we had just seen.

Can Australia give Don the time and support he needs? Can Australia help Josh and the Mithaka protect a site which is more important for the understanding of humans than any other on Earth? Here people lived and traded and performed ceremony for that trade. And perhaps they performed those complex operations before any other humans and all of it within the arch of spiritual codes.

Yes, there is a massive ceremonial site above the mines where trader and buyer gathered to honour the trade. I think of that interaction all the time. The ceremony site extends for over 2 kilometres.

A testament to the bond between those on both sides of the transactions are the standing stones marking the sites of each mine. They signal a proprietary interest to indicate to other miners that this site was occupied.

Of course, the words buyer and proprietary are not suitable, but what words do we use for a trade where the miner wanted to trade with other people in a comfortable exchange instead of enriching him or herself. There is no castle here, no moat, no treasure hoard, no army, and the mines themselves, of such obvious importance, are protected by a simple standing stone. No razor wire, no alarms, no guards, because in this society theft was unthinkable. Think how that one social rule would reshape the bible.

I rolled into Windorah well after dark and the affable archae-ologists were deep in conversation and beers. There was talk of their vegetation studies, bird and animal surveys, test cores, population estimates; all fascinating stuff, but I was thinking of a little girl playing with pebbles as she replicated the living pattern of her people.

Australia, the world, you will be astounded by that little girl's vision because she was able to replicate the boundaries of her exist-ence where there was no army, no prison, no poverty. Does the world need to consider the possibility that humans have the ability to live like that? Does a kangaroo jump?

I slept fitfully in the caravan park, rocked to the core by the little girl's vision of life. I got up at four and began driving south-east, unnerved by the cattle and roos looming out of the dark. I think I saw a bilby or was it a large bandicoot? I have never seen a creature with such disproportionately large ears. It comforted me to know that, whatever it was, it existed. I was hungry as hell because I had been too late for the pub's kitchen last night.

I arrived at the quiet little town of Quilpie, but nothing was open except a tiny coffee caravan. The affable owner served me coffee and a lovely toasted sandwich which I enjoyed in the company of a whimsical couple who seemed not to have a worry in the world.

Drove on, drove on and eventually made it to Charleville where I saw a sign for Golders of Roma. To watch football and cricket at my house I have to use a satellite which means I get Alice Springs Imparja TV and all their ads are for cattle drench, water tanks, mine supplies and instructions to wash my face and blow my nose. I also get ads for Golders of Roma. The owner and his daughters are legendary dags, so I made up my mind I had to shop there.

I left carrying a bag with shorts in Queensland Origin rugby colours, a shirt in a maroon the colour of a mad steer's eyes and pants charcoal enough to allow for bushfire wood collection without totally destroying their newness. Little remembrances make me very happy. At last I have been to Golders of Roma, even if it was in Charleville.

I got as far as Dalby and collapsed at a motel where Jane Grieve, the motel manager and author, recognised me and wanted to talk Aboriginal history. She had written a book, *In Stockmen's Footsteps*, about the Stockmen's Hall of Fame, so it was a difficult conversation, but they are the conversations we must have. Building trenches is not a viable human discourse.

Jane served me a lovely curry and seemed generally interested in Aboriginal opinion but my eyes were dropping out of my head and I slept soundly, dreaming of Don's stone walls and his Coolabah tree.

I had to get driving again early to hand back the car in Coffs Harbour. I stayed that night in Sydney's very forgettable airport hotel. The suburb is a tangle of highways and disconnection but, fortunately, I had the desert memories to sift and understand.

The journey was the most important in a life of many journeys and I'm hoping my mere words can tempt Australians, black and white, to care for the country and the spiritual significance her First People had built upon her.

Lyn picked me up from Merimbula and when I got to her place all I wanted was rest and reflection but a kid went missing in Gipsy Point so the whole town turned out for the search. He was found safely but the buzz of adrenalin seared for hours afterward.

I went to Lyn's fire control meeting to support her and brother, Graham Moore, but the caution and defensiveness of the authorities makes you feel that nothing will happen unless people start it themselves. Thank goodness for Lyn's grace and persistence. She is a good person and loves her Country so much she is prepared to attend a dozen boring meetings a week to try and make Mallacoota safe, copping all the bickering and meanness in return.

Next morning, she wrote about Jitti Jitti's insistent conversation at dawn. 'Are you sure, Jitti Jitti, that you need to drag us from our sleep or are you just spreading rumours? The wattlebird is demanding, "Wake up, wake up." Might as well get everybody moving as it's too early to sip nectar. Now, who's upset the plovers? They've been alarmed half the night but are still offended as the gentle kangaroos move through the mist. There will be no return to sleep now as the currawongs chorus begins, the call and response a cheery barachello.'

The Jitti Jitti is certainly persistent at this time of year, as if protecting, or contemplating, a nest. It calls tut twitty twit it over and over again, quite distinct from its usual call. The currawongs have flocked in a big group and the plovers are excitable, so I think their young are down near the horse paddock. Every time they call Pippin goes on alert and scans the farm for threat.

Possum Skin

I did the dreaded 4 am drive in the dark to catch the first plane in a series of flights to Adelaide. The early Merimbula connection was late, making the whole travel a tense rush.

I helped Damo and Bec from Warndu launch their new cookbook with the irrepressible Costa Georgiades. It would have been nice to share some yarns and a few beers but I had to creep off to bed.

It was Lyn's birthday and I left her a present, a rug I bought at the South Australian Museum last time we were there. It's an ochre

Possum skin rug

rug and reminded her of her beloved desert. She bought me a book on Australian animals so we could identify a strange creature leaping around my barbeque.

On day two of the Warndu gig, Costa and I did an early show at Plant 3 in Bowden. I dobbed in a couple of good jokes, well they cheered me because I felt I had been dragging my feet. That night we did a job for the Kaurna community but it was freezing cold and I was propped up on the back of someone's old ute. It had been set up beautifully but the wind was freezing my back.

Someone saw what was going on and jumped on to the ute and draped a rug around my shoulders. I looked down at the hem and saw that it was a possum skin and that the inside had been inscribed. It was the first time I had worn one. I have seen plenty of people wear them but to me it seems a bit stagey and disrespectful. My family made me one for my seventieth birthday but I don't wear it out of respect. It is my winter blanket and I get so much joy in the knowledge that my family are keeping me warm.

When Aunty Joy Wandin, senior Wurundjeri elder, wears one I feel pride in her right to do so and I have seen Ken Wyatt wear a kangaroo skin with rare dignity, but sometimes I see people posture in them and it turns my stomach. The garment has huge spiritual significance and needs to be respected. It is not to be used as a political tool like a prime minister donning a hard hat and high vis vest to demonstrate his allegiance to the working class.

When I got back to the farm from South Australia it was another misty morning and Lyn and I watched Bunjil circling the top of the south paddock before it landed on something and struggled to lift it into the air. After many attempts it was able to get the creature aloft and disappeared. It looked like the catch, Bodalla (wallaby), was dead before capture but it made us wonder if there was already a young Bunjil in the nest. Well, that meal would certainly keep it busy for a few days.

We went to Merimbula and had lunch at the aquarium to celebrate our birthdays. A beautiful meal and a chance for us to catch up on each other's news after such busy days.

I was asked to do a program for SBS on identity but Blackfellas warned me against it. They suspected a contest between dark and pale Blackfellas. But I thought that it was a chance to set the record straight. I spent about four hours talking through my family history with SBS researchers. They seemed genuinely interested so I sent photos and documents and felt that nothing could go wrong.

Off I went to Sydney, but SBS used none of what I gave them, instead preferring the rumour and assumption of the right-wing press. I was really devastated and disappointed that with all the work that needs to be done in our communities we would waste our time on this trivia. I felt sorry for some of the other participants who also thought it was a chance to have their say.

How wrong we were. The 'real' blacks were on one side of the room and we were on the other. I wonder if I have ever been more disillusioned. I gave really precise information about my family, so proud am I of their survival, but sadly they used none of that.

I also calculated the percentage of blood in my family and the difficulty this raises in community. These are important points to consider because as more and more Australians find black relatives these issues have to be considered before we become a bunch of wannabes, but no, SBS chose a sensationalist and divisive path. Trumpist.

Definitions of Aboriginality need to be understood by everyone. I don't believe in self-identification, I think people ought to be able to provide some documentary evidence of their identity, but I also know that some people who were taken away have not one skerrick of evidence. A man approached me at a function in Perth last month to share his identity confusion with me. What he didn't know was that I identified him as Aboriginal the moment I entered the room. There was no mistaking it, but he had no birth certificate and wasn't even sure of his birthday. Stolen Generation.

All of these issues could have built a really constructive documentary, could have drawn people toward an understanding of identity, not urged them toward scorn and contempt. And what will happen to Aboriginal people who are made afraid to identify, will we lose their contribution to the Aboriginal family? I feel the same way about non-Aboriginal people; they are not going away so they have to be encouraged to identify with the land or otherwise how can they care for her? They will be restless spirits forever feeling at a distance from their home.

I knew the show's director so was doubly broken by the way an important opportunity was lost. Never again. There are people who reckon we should sue when this sort of thing happens. What, and spend the rest of our lives in court to change nothing? The tethered bear being drained of bile to please a conspiracy myth! No thanks.

The day after the SBS show I went to see performances of my play at the Barracks in order to support the cast and company, but it meant I had to change my flight from 2 pm to 6.30 pm and of course it was late. One of the passengers went through the wrong door so we had to wait for her. She'd just had a hip operation and so it was a long wait. Once on the tarmac we waited for clearance but time crept toward Sydney's air curfew and eventually the flight was cancelled and we were ushered off the plane and had to walk back to the airport. Which was locked.

Once we were let into the terminal we were told to leave the building. No help whatsoever. It was midnight by now and no motel rooms left. One passenger rang a number on a hotel website and was put through to Los Angeles where a cheery person told us that there were three rooms left. It was news to the hotel clerk but those rooms were found and nine of us were able to bunk in them.

It seemed like a horrible way to punish passengers for Rex Airlines' failure but, once again, the human spirit showed itself. In the middle of all this travail and uncertainty we were waiting helplessly in a motel lobby and the lady with the crook hip looked around at the decor and said, 'This is nice, isn't it?' You had to love her spirit.

Once I got back to the farm I spent days doing interviews with earnest university students wanting to talk permaculture, Aboriginal sovereignty, agricultural sustainability and climate change. I work one day a week for Melbourne University and it gives me the opportunity to work with this generation and it inspires hope.

I had to leave the farm once again to do the commemoration at Beth Gott's memorial in Melbourne. Beth did all the early work on Aboriginal use of Yam Daisy and was important in helping me get elements of *Dark Emu* botanically correct. She was gentle but persistent in her corrections and I appreciated her stern support.

The room was full of researchers and Blackfellas whose names were lit in neon for me as their work had also contributed so much to *Dark Emu*. When the wine and Saos were being passed around I collected a group of them together and asked what they thought of the idea of Aboriginal accomplishment.

I was prepared for them to nitpick their way through my work, as some others have done, but one said Australia had a problem with the words village and digging when it was applied to Aboriginal people.

It was a very concise way of showing the gaps in the history accepted by many Australians. Other researchers chimed in with news of the most recent research and archaeology and I was shocked at the amount of new information supporting Aboriginal technical expertise.

I asked about Jim Bowler's research. Jim has just finished an excavation at Point Richie, Warrnambool. Jim was at the forefront of the Mungo man and Mungo lady research which had transformed science's understanding of the age of Aboriginal occupation of Australia. Jim's new science, however, was suggesting an occupation of a site at Warrnambool of 120,000 years.

Once again, I was prepared for the gathered experts to scoff but, instead, they gave intriguing commentary that only insiders could give. They pointed out the quibbles that some scientists have about the theory, but also suggested that a lot of that hesitancy comes from a race wedded to the idea of Western superiority. Beth would have loved it because it was right up her alley, but she will have to settle for the fact that we were doing it at her wake.

The Starling

Starlings arrive at the farm around mid-October every year. I am not welcoming. I shoot at them with an air rifle. I don't hit many but they are aware of my displeasure. They are such beautiful, character-filled beings, but so were Governor Phillip and Captain Cook according to their mothers.

A small group arrives and usually sits in surveillance mode on the old dead tree for an hour before venturing to feed on the pasture.

The way the birds strut is very distinctive and assertive, they are a wonderful creature, but I know that if I let them stay there will be a few hundred arriving the next day. I have to make them feel unwelcome or it will be Captain Cook all over again.

On the road again. I had to fly to Sydney to help Dean Kelly, Aunty Barb Simms and other La Perouse mob run some whale tours outside Sydney Harbour. I had a chance to talk with Gurandgi Del Ella and his new partner Chelise. It is always so inspiring to hear about the work our young people are doing on behalf of our communities. It is truly the highlight of my life.

Aunty Barb was really complimentary about my books and after the SBS horror it felt like I was living in two opposed universes. We saw whales and we sang their songs to the other passengers, many of whom were from other countries. I look forward to the day when all Australians will be familiar with this Country's songs for the whale.

The eye of Gurawul (Image reproduced with permission from Yuin Gurandji senior men)

Spring

Dingo

*The vigour of spring is all around us: the unfurling tree fern frond,
the energy that pushes the orchids delicate stem through hard crust,
the arrival of cuckoos. The urgency of growth and desire.*

Red in Tooth and Claw

No problems getting home for once and got straight into picking up rotted eucalyptus mulch from Gipsy Point and spreading it on my house gardens.

I feed a male King Parrot irregular meals of sunflower seeds because he asks so politely, talking to me in such a conversational and confiding tone.

He might be polite but he doesn't like it when another male tries to intrude. If the Rainbow Lorikeets scare him away from the seed he will search the windows of the house until he finds me and asks for intercession. It is such a peculiar relationship. The Rainbow Lorikeets screech like urchin bandits while the King Parrot whispers secrets. I value the company of all of them.

Three baby swallows are sitting on the gutter above the back door near the nest where they were born a few weeks ago. Every time I leave the house I am dive-bombed by the parents. Have they forgotten that it's me who turns on the outside light to keep them warm on frosty nights?

I woke to thunderous rain and began to worry about the roads. The Striped Marsh Frogs are loving the wet weather but I'm concerned about the gravel. Water is already gushing out of the Water Ribbon dam.

I looked out the window and the Buru were standing erect and switching their heads about looking for something. The horses were on hyper alert. While we were making breakfast, Lyn saw some Mirrigan (dingoes) down near the flooding dam. We have been seeing Mirrigan up by the northern gate for a few weeks and this looks like the same pair, solid golden animals, fit and assured.

The commotion amongst the Buru continued but their focus shifted from one side of the farm to the other. They were mightily confused. One small joey got separated from its mother and just stood by the BBQ seemingly immobilised by fear and uncertainty.

Then we saw two dingoes charge at a mob, switching them back and forth across the paddock. Finally, a young Buru was isolated and the male dog attacked him. The roo was brought down but in a mighty struggle freed itself and took off further into the swamp. I lost sight of it but could hear it splashing through the shallow water. The female dog reappeared and she circled around the edge of the swamp while the male drove the roo onwards. It looked like a well-rehearsed plan.

I had to go to work but knew that I would find the roo on the edge of the swamp when I got a chance to get down there later in the day. Around midday I saw the first Bunjil fly into a tree at the edge of the swamp and guessed that the dogs had got their fill and loped away to rest in the forest.

Later Whistling Kites arrived too and then a second Bunjil. After work I walked down to the swamp and found the poor Buru with its ears eaten off. Mirrigan often drags a Buru down by the ear to immobilise it.

A few years ago Vicky Shukuroglou and I saw a roo at Namadgi National Park that had both ears eaten off. The Park Ranger told the story of how Vincent had survived two attacks by dingoes but as a result his head now had the appearance of a camel.

The stomach cavity of the Buru killed this morning had been opened and the intestines removed and the heart and liver eaten. The birds waited petulantly while I inspected the animal, but as soon as I moved away, they glided back to their meal.

It was both sad and thrilling. Sad to see a young animal hunted, but thrilling to see the natural order in operation. The Mirrigan were casually organised in the beginning and then ruthless in their execution.

The rain continued and the river rose quickly. I'm sure Mirrigan ran the roo into the swamp deliberately because the extra depth would slow it down.

I dug drains during the heaviest rain because that's when you can see what needs to be done to guide the water safely.

I was drenched when I got back to the house and while I waited to dry off I took Dad's old spirit level apart. No one on the farm will use it because the lenses are cloudy. I washed the glass and reinstalled them. It brought me very close to Dad and was a lovely thing to do as the rain hammered down.

When the rain eased I went down to see what was happening at Mirrigan's kill site. The eagles and kites were sharing the carcass in a prickly arrangement and didn't appreciate the disturbance of my company. Now the Buru's face had been eaten off but there was no sign of Mirrigan.

While I was down at the swamp I noticed that *Nadgee* had slipped her forward mooring as well. She was gone. If she had drifted downstream she could end up out in the ocean. I walked the bank of Yumburra Creek with my heart in my mouth and then caught a glimpse of her nuzzling the bank.

I paddled out to her on the faithful blue board and tied her up to the bank and put a long lead rope on her bow and threw the anchor off the stern so she'd ride in midstream. It was such a relief to find her because my heart would have been very sore if my carelessness had allowed her to be lost.

The swallows had collected in a large group and were feeding while hovering close to the grass and sometimes brushing it with their feet. Were they taking advantage of insects which are trying to get away from the surface moisture in the paddock? It is a plan as deliberate and well-executed as the Mirrigan hunt.

I had to drive to Pambula to talk to Sydney University students who had been planning to stay at the farm but their vehicles couldn't have coped with the crossings which were now up to the running board of the ute. Bit sloppy in the cab.

It was a good yarn with the students but it was getting dark by the time I returned to the farm and I had to get out to *Nadgee* and bring her back to the jetty as the flood was dropping and I didn't want her to get snagged amongst the riverbank Melaleucas. I was wet by the time I finished but there's an idiot in me that loves the flood dramas.

Bunjil was sitting on the carcass of the young roo and stared at me in defiance. I heard the first Scarlet Honeyeater of the season, a real indication of changing weather. The Golden Whistlers, Black-faced Cuckoo-shrikes and the Rufous Whistlers were all back in residence too and I rejoiced in their return.

On Friday 28 October I had to fly to Orange to deliver the NSW History Society Annual address. It meant leaving at 4 am in the dark. The mist was so heavy that the headlights were almost useless and I ran into the branches of a fallen tree before I had even seen it. The slap against the side of the car was mighty and it dented panels and wiped out the mirror and most of the electronics. I was already late and so drove on hoping the car wouldn't stall.

I arrived just in time to catch the plane at Merimbula but was so rushed I couldn't even inspect the damage to the poor old ute. I was very lucky the branch hadn't been a few centimetres higher or it would have come through the windscreen at eye level.

I got to Orange in convoluted fashion and the presentation I called The White Orchid of Melbourne was very well received.

A whole bunch of historians and archaeologists were there and their enthusiasm buoyed me. The Aboriginal community were fantastic too and we had a long yarn afterwards. The local kids who have been kicked out of school made me a painted boomerang. I was really moved by their thoughtfulness and support. It means so much to me given the trolls on social media are so vicious.

Diuris similar to the endangered fragrant White Orchid

Orange Museum was hosting a local Aboriginal story exhibition and it was great to have a couple of hours to enjoy it. Two of Lyn's desert painting mates gave me a lift to the airport and I asked Don to look in on the kids who made the boomerang, to make sure they were supported by the Education Department. That's the point at which we need to spend the money and time on young people, not after they have lost their way.

I then flew to Brisbane in time to work on my presentation for the Harlan IV agricultural conference. The University of Queensland were doing a full exposition of their work at Mithaka. This was our chance to speak to the profession about the grindstone mines and their significance.

I think we were all anxious that the presentation was as thorough as we could make it. There wasn't a big crowd but they were all academics active in the area so it felt worthwhile.

Out in the Convention Hall there were several Aboriginal food producers and we had a good old yarn and they loaded me up with jars of their produce and t-shirts. Those are the moments that keep me going, the community sticking together.

It was a long trip back home in the battered ute and, in a daze, I took the boat down to Gipsy Point to watch the Melbourne Cup at the house of Libby and Mitch, our good friends and neighbours. It was great to talk boats, fish, gardens and fowl and nobody seemed to notice that the TV was on the wrong channel. The Cup was won by a horse so we just shrugged and got on with small town chat. I don't socialise often so it was good to catch up with people from the district.

There is always work on the farm. Heaps of it. I was working on a new garden but also had to repair a pipe and then pick up soil with the tractor to fill in potholes which had got worse during the rains. While I was doing those jobs I noticed another plover sitting on eggs. Tractor work can be hard and tedious but there is always something happening in the natural world and the time flies.

When I had a chance for a cup of coffee, Terry and I had an hour where we could yarn about the culture and the lore jobs we have to do for Uncle Max. A brother from the Australian National University rang later to talk similar things. It was a full and rich day but I was exhausted by sunset and I struggle to get excited about cooking a meal on days like that.

In the morning the swallows were doing their butterfly hover over the tops of the grass again. I am fascinated by their various feeding patterns and how they work together like a large family.

The roos have been scarce since the dingo attack but as I drove out of the farm to attend the Twofold Aboriginal Corporation fortnightly meeting, I saw all the Buru hiding out in the forest where they have more protection.

When I got back home I worked on the boat motor which has started playing up again. While I was working on the motor I noticed a large male deer in the swamp.

I cleaned up and picked up Lyn so we could drive up to Mudgee to do a food festival presentation for Sharon Winsor, a sister I've known for decades and who has joined the Black Duck board despite being incredibly busy with her own business. It was lovely spending time with her family again as they danced and sang cultural songs. One of the dancers had a long yarn with us. She's so excited about graduating as a lawyer next week.

The drive home was long and hard. I have to avoid doing those long stretches in the future. Too dangerous.

We had the Wadawoorong and World Wildlife Fund mob arrive for some workshops on the farm. It was wonderful to work with more Aboriginal people interested in culture and food. We cooked a wonderful meal up at Bun Bun Gungwan using all our own ingredients.

We all continued the farm tour the next day, sharing knowledge about the plants and culture.

Sharon's family of dancers

That night Chris cooked his famous kangaroo stew and the rest of us did the bread and dessert. It's a big job cooking for twenty people on the open fire but the conversation while we do it is always enriched by the expectation of filling our bellies from Country.

A few weeks back the fellas found a freshly run over echidna on their way to work and as we had a burn pile going we threw the animal on to the flames after removing forty or so quills to use in our artwork. They are a really fatty animal which helps them cook moistly and the flesh really is delicious. It has the texture and taste of pork but I think it is sweeter. Waste not, want not.

I picked some cunjim winyu (Yuin language for 'salty sun', a little herb that grows on the margin of the salt swamp) and sea celery, fresh herbs that grow in our wetlands, for our research manager Cheryl Taylor to analyse for us at the CSIRO. I sent some of our wattle

Eating cumbungi

seed up as well so that we can sell our produce on the market with confidence. I can't see that we will ever make much money from our growing but we will be introducing new foods to the market. New for the market but old for the country.

Jitti Jitti is really loud at dawn these days and the Red Wattlebird joins in. The familiarity of it and the subtle changes in their behaviour draws me ever closer to these wild creatures. Jitti Jitti is such a people person but for the wattlebird we just grow plants it likes. The bird is watchful and knowing of our habits but never seeks greater intimacy, whereas the King Parrot will sit on my shoulder and tell me fibs about the Rainbow Lorikeets.

There is a Yumburra (Black Duck) and Binyaroo (cormorant) feeding together in the top dam. The cormorant has been there for days so it encourages me to think that dropping logs around the edges and allowing reeds to grow has created a healthy habitat for aquatic animals. When I first arrived at the farm this dam was a sterile basin.

Jitti Jitti (Leonie Daws)

Boats

Chris Harris helped me identify the problem with *Nadgee*'s motor and so I went into town and bought a set of spark plugs and now she runs as sweet as a bird. It's a relief because *Nadgee* gives me so much freedom of movement and the absolute pleasure of being on the water. Since a child I have been bewitched by the action of boats, their buoyancy and liveliness. It is a completely different feeling to being on land.

As a boy I used to lay in the bow of *Coonah*, the little rowboat Dad and I made. I would listen to small waves slapping and knocking at the timber and drift off to sleep in a trance of peace. I learnt so much about myself in that boat and its echoes can still be seen in my poetry and stories, the world of wild gentleness.

We were cold stony broke when Dad bought that boat. Like many of our purchases it was actually a barter. One of Dad's mates made do-it-yourself boat kits and he had one that had been cut out incorrectly. Dad swapped a window renovation on that bloke's house for the boat pack. He cut the boat pieces down by a few centimetres and made the rest fit together. She was beautiful.

I spent days poring over paint charts. I wanted her to represent Maran (seagull) and Gadu (ocean). I got the white and grey just right but when it came to the beak and legs I was torn. Red didn't seem right with the other colours so I chose the yellow of Grandfather Sun. She looked beautiful to my eyes and I loved her so dearly.

Dad and I made a trailer out of old bike wheels and frames and I could haul her down to the beach on my own. I spent days in her, mostly alone, diving and fishing. Dad was as generous and thoughtful a man as you will find but, even though he worked on cray boats on King Island, he forgot to include an anchor. One day I found myself in the shipping lane in Port Phillip Bay and had to row like steam to get out of there. I couldn't rest because the tide just took me further south. I rowed all the way back to Mornington, my arms nearly falling off.

I made my own anchor out of a shoe last and a length of rope. We had to pull it to pieces every time Dad put new soles on our shoes. I can still smell the leather and glue he used. He boiled resin beads to fix shoes and furniture. It was the work of alchemy, and I thought of him like that, a magician.

I'm not nearly as adept as Dad but the fact I can fix things is a testament to how closely I watched his hands.

Binyaroo and Bitheega

Binyaroo was still feeding in the dam and I feel enormous happiness that I have helped create a place from which she can feed herself. I showed her to Noel and Trish Butler who were here to cook for the Mallacoota Wild Harvest Seafood Festival.

All the Black Duck mob helped Noel do his presentation dinner. My job was to scrub the Bimbla (Blood Mussels) and oysters, which meant I was on my knees, head over a bowl, but it made me invisible to the crowd so I had an armchair seat to their conversations. Writer's Gold.

People are stunned by Noel's hot oysters, the taste of the sea is in them, the juice like liquor. I do mussels like that too; to drink the brine from the shell is one of the great luxuries of our lives.

A Maori diving mate taught me how to eat Kina (sea urchins) too. When I come back from a dive I sit in a rock pool and crack open an urchin and sluice the shell halves and eat the roe. It is as decadent as life can get. Years ago, Gurandgi were diving for Walkun (abalone) and I showed them the urchin trick and we sat around in the warm water of Green Cape gorging on shellfish roe. We never drink on the eleven days of our camps, and it rarely bothers me, too busy, but on that day I was thinking a dry sparkling wine would have been perfect.

Because I just wrote the above I indulged in the luxury of a dive at the Tura Beach rockpool. It's a steep climb down to it and I am so nervous of having a fall and breaking something these days that I crabbed my way down to the water. It was a superb day and the water was jade green from the brightness of the sun.

Once in the water the old physical freedom returned and I revelled in being a tourist in that other world, gliding over kelps and sponges, cavers and crevices. I feel so at ease in that world.

I pulled a big urchin from a cave and cracked it open in a little channel as the waves dandled me in a bed of kelp. The roe was delicious and I lay back in the kelp as relaxed as I have been for years.

I got dressed and as I was getting ready to leave a bloke came around a headland in the rocks and stopped dead. I realised he'd seen the Black Duck badge on the shoulder of my shirt and he must have thought I was a fisho or park ranger. I wonder what he had in his bag.

I have dived for seafood most of my life and have come across all sorts of poachers. Years ago at Cape Otway I met one underwater. He had a long-hooked spear and we looked at each other for a few seconds before he turned away. I later found the spear he had dropped and later still the skid marks of his tyres as he left the car park in a hurry.

The market system has hiked the price of abalone and crayfish to such an extent that criminals have been attracted to the industry and the sea is now so plundered that fish and crustacea are in very serious decline.

In the fifties Dad used to buy two crayfish wrapped in newspaper for two bob (shillings) and in the seventies my brother-in-law and I used to catch crays in rockpools with a stick wrapped in panty hose without getting our feet wet. Those days are long gone, not because the animals have stopped breeding, but because the Western market system has no respect for the earth or ocean.

Cleaning the Fridge

Richmond got beaten in our AFL semi-final by a few points. We should have won it but the goal umpire robbed us blind.

Never mind, Lyn and I went down to the Water Ribbon Dam and recorded Eastern Dwarf Tree Frogs, Peron's Tree Frog, Common Eastern Froglet, Striped Marsh Frog and others and contributed the data to FrogID Week. You probably didn't know there was a FrogID Week but I didn't think we would ever be beaten by a Queensland football team either.

To celebrate I cleaned the fridge.

I also started to clean up the caravan because Ken Bridle is interested in buying it. I taught Ken, so he doesn't know much, but he's a very good farmer and decent fella. He helped me during the fires and taught me a trick about water pumps for which I am very grateful.

I bought a little pop-up van to live in while I had a new floor put into the house. My kids have used it on holidays and two farm workers have lived in her for months. But Ken wanted her more than I did. So, I washed down the old van all the while remembering how good she had been to me.

Lyn says the lyrebirds at her place have been getting raucous and a fully plumaged male dances in a shimmering feather veil watched by females and juveniles. The birds appear on Lyn's verandah to ransack her potted plants and have nested around the house including the garage of the bed and breakfast next door. My lyrebirds stick to the bush around the property. They don't like to cross the open spaces of the paddocks, too vulnerable to Bunjil and sparrowhawks and dingoes.

I took Noel and Trish for a boat ride. They love boats and Trish is an ardent swimmer. I have worried about them ever since they lost their house in the fires. Bad luck has pursued them even after such loss. I like to see them relax and water Country is a great healer.

I showed them the ochre hills where I get ceremonial ochre for Gurandgi and some of the Aboriginal dance troupes. Being on Country like that is deeply relaxing and I wanted them to know where that ochre came from. Passing on the lore.

Emus, Old Brass and Fire

Allan Clarke, director of the ABC film *The Dark Emu Story*, came to the farm to talk through script issues. I am keen that the archaeology behind the book is well represented, particularly as the work at Mithaka, provoked by *Dark Emu*, has such far-reaching implications for humanity.

After Allan left I worked on my new gardens. I have been adding nutrients to the gardens with mulch created at Lyn's after the fires. It's heavy work and I find it frustrating at how my stamina has dwindled over the last few years. (This year my doctor discovered I had a blocked artery. Drilling that out has made a big difference.)

While I was working, a Melbourne University forestry researcher turned up to talk about forest thinning. She was very enthusiastic about our method but I think she stands a snowball's chance in hell of convincing her male superiors. I suspect they do small projects like this as window dressing for the horror they have created.

The wattlebirds and Rainbow Lorikeets are competing for the grevilleas. The wattlebird grew very impatient and flew beneath the lorikeet and latched on to its tail. Sugar eaters are very feisty.

I'd been working on the grapevine netting and track clearing and then writing a recipe for our bread for *The Australian*. While reading their paper that morning, however, I discovered more racial slurs against me, so I rang the editor to withdraw the recipe. I was happy to promote Indigenous food but not in a paper where some of the writing owes more to the Rottweiler than to true journalism.

Anyway, the recipe is not complicated. We combine about 50 per cent baking flour with 50 per cent of our own flour, either Kangaroo and Spear, or Mitchell and Button. Chris adds yeast and salt while Lyn uses her sourdough starter. We have a breadmaker but often cook it in a camp oven or straight on the coals. The aroma is a revelation. We sell our flour on our Black Duck website or at the farm gate.

I worked on removing saplings overhanging the track through the national park. The regrowth after the fires was incredible, but now those young trees are falling and blocking the road and creating firebomb conditions in the bush. February 2024 will be the start of many fires. We should have been cool burning in the parks and forests

Camp oven bread

just weeks after the 2019 fires but now it will be very difficult. To drive from the farm, where we practise cool burning, to the national park is a real indication of the benefits of traditional burning. It worries me that our farm access is through such a dense tangle of regrowth.

It was an incredibly windy day on 21 November and I stayed inside fixing brass handles to an old chest I bought Maggie and Rosie's Antiques in Bega. I use it as a coffee table but it is hard to move and looks a bit blank, characterless. The handles dress it up a bit and make it easier to shift and it gives me an inordinate amount of pleasure to see the transformation of a very ordinary bit of furniture.

I did a bit of work on the boat after the wind abated and I was accompanied by a Gunyu family. The young swan was all tan and fluffy, obviously too young to fly, and the parents paddled sedately down the creek and around the corner, out of range of my knocking and clanking in the boat.

I flew to Sydney early on 23 November and it was a long day of filming. My good friend Liz Warning is the researcher for *The Dark Emu Story* and her presence reassured me. I am quite sick of the whole thing, but Liz tells me that Lyn was fantastic in the piece she did to camera.

Liz has been providing me with research papers on archaeological sites for years. She was quick to understand how this new knowledge could transform Australian understanding of its history. If we were able escape the closed gate of the naysayers.

The filming required me to fly to Melbourne to get more footage at Alia and Charlee's school. Marnie has put in a lot of work in the food garden there and I was able to show the kids all the Munyang and Murnong the garden had produced. I love that little school. I have visited it often as the grandkids have progressed through the grades. The central hall area is real old-world education architecture, completely charming.

It's a really well-run school and I never fail to be warmed by the inquisitive nature of the kids and the support the teachers give them. One deeply troubled girl found it too difficult to join the group being filmed but was fascinated by the camera gear and so the teachers and film crew ran her through a private lesson, just the way a compassionate school and world should operate.

We then went over to Melbourne University and I talked to the agriculture students under the gaze of the film crew. Afterwards Marnie and I had a lunch just to ourselves. I always appreciate those times when I can have the kids to myself.

I remember fishing with Marnie in Smellie's Inlet a couple of decades ago. She just prattled away and hauled in fish after fish as if

Lyn faces the camera for the filming of The Dark Emu Story *(Liz Warning)*

it was the only way fishing could be done. I loved it. Once when Jack and I went over to Tasmania to research the family tree we had some beers and scallops on a houseboat in the Huon River. I still think of it as one of the best afternoons of my life.

Back home I helped Lyn work in her garden. When we had finished I returned to the farm by boat but as I approached my jetty I noticed there was a water dragon basking there, the first time I had seen one on my own jetty. I was so encouraged by that sighting.

The film crew arrived later that day so it was intense concentration again. All the time we were working I could hear this year's young Bunjil calling, kissook kissook kissook, while the parents glided over the duck pen avid-eyed.

The young Pipits were working the edges of the slashed paddock picking up grass heads and insects. The bird activity kept me patient during the protracted tedium of the filming.

The script called for a harvest of Munyang and Murnong. The tubers were wonderful and it felt like we were showing Australia the future of their diet and gardens. Perennial vegetables; no poison, little water, no pesticides.

The evening was gorgeous and just on dusk I saw a Garramagang (magpie) scream around the corner of the house in pursuit of some small bird. It was a real dashing and twisting dogfight. I couldn't see what kind of bird it was or why the Garramagang was so intent but, in any case, the little bird managed to escape.

That night I was overwhelmed with Gurandgi business as we tried to reconcile ourselves to the passing of Uncle Max almost twelve months ago. His loss has created a huge gap and we have filled the void with disquiet. It is exhausting, but we continue because the old man anticipated all the unrest and gave us clear instructions as to how it must be handled. We persevere for the sake of the ancient lore.

Early Summer

*The grass turns golden tinged with russet and in late afternoon
you can smell it ripening. The whole hillside dances with wind in
the grass and we are reminded that we are not the first to look
across the land and imagine bread.*

Queensberry Rules

The first day of summer and the young male Buru box each other at dawn. They are holding their heads out of the way too. To protect their eyes? Males have much stronger forearms than the females and we speculate on why they tip their heads back out of the way. I have heard many theories but it is most probably to protect their eyes.

The Garramagang (magpie) chased a little bird again this morning but it looked more like displeasure than hunting. I think the small bird was a Yellow-rumped Thornbill. The thornbill nests in the callistemon near the kitchen window and feeds in that tree and the Lucerne tree in the backyard. I couldn't see how that would make the Garramagang cranky. Surely the thornbill wasn't competing for food or nesting material. I have seen a butcherbird attack, kill and flay a Red-browed Finch and I know Garramagang can eat nestlings of other birds, but to chase and kill, I'm not sure.

The politics of the garden is fascinating. After the chase the thornbill flew to the top of the dead tree in front of the house. It is a mystery.

There are a few frictions amongst the farm employees too and we are hoping it can be sorted out. I worried about the tensions as I drove to catch the plane to Sydney. When I arrived I blobbed out with a meal and a beer while watching cricket. Sport is really calming for me. I take the results seriously when I have a vested interest but if they lose it is just a game. No one dies. Because I have played so much sport I get enjoyment from watching the tactics, some of which I used to employ, but at about 10 per cent the skill level. The abilities of top-flight sportspeople make my jaw drop. Watching any of the Rioli family playing AFL makes me marvel at their athleticism. I treasure a t-shirt their aunty gave me forty years ago. It is so old it has fallen to pieces but I use the logo of the Tiwi Tigers as my computer cleaning cloth.

I thought Maurice Rioli Snr was the best footballer I had ever seen. When I saw how quickly he understood a play situation and then spun and weaved a way through the congestion it just made me shake my head. I would try to emulate it at training for my own club but I just didn't have it. My brain didn't respond quickly enough and my legs weren't nimble enough. Sad but true.

I had more success at cricket but enjoyed it half as much. But today, sport is a solace for me as the rest of my life is so full of responsibility and threat.

We filmed *The Dark Emu Story* all day in the Mitchell Library and it gave me the chance to read the original notebooks of Sir Thomas Mitchell and the first editions of journals by Mitchell, Sturt and Grey. It really fascinates me what these people recorded and what our early educators and historians deemed unfit for our children to learn.

The next morning, I shopped for Christmas at some kind of mall. I shop quickly and efficiently and really enjoy thinking about what individuals will like. I like second-hand shops most of all because you can match a quirky object to a quirky person. Sometimes I get strange looks from my family on Christmas day but I know I'm right, they just haven't realised who they are yet!

I headed back to the wonderful Mitchell Library but I dragged my feet because I was going to film with the anthropologist linguist Peter Sutton. I found it hard to believe how rude he was and how resistant to the idea of Aboriginal achievement. We looked at the same texts and what I saw as genius he dismissed as aberration.

I was unsettled and deeply disillusioned by this day. I am attacked so frequently I was hoping not to experience it again in my second favourite library in Australia. When I got home Lindsay was replacing some posts in the horse paddock. He is one of my best friends but I just couldn't bring myself to go down and help.

Instead, I listened to the first Striated Pardalotes of the season and later went and had a swim to calm myself. My neighbour Kate dropped off some toolbags she had sewn to the design my mother made to hold Dad's chisels. I still have a couple of the original bags and so I got Kate to make me a dozen for Christmas presents for the family. I am so pleased with them that I have asked her to make me another twenty and I'm going to give one to each of the Black Duck workers and board and each of the senior Gurandgi.

My mother was an extraordinary woman. She was deaf, blind and epileptic but her spirit compensated for all of it. She only went blind later in life, as a result of the epilepsy perhaps, but she embraced her new condition and took on executive roles in the Royal Victorian Institute for the Blind and taught herself to play lawn bowls and won several gold medals for Australia at the Paralympics overseas and in Australia.

But those things weren't the half of her. She had the biggest heart. We always had people living with us that Mum was looking after. We lived for a time in an old house where three rooms were built directly on to the dirt but that didn't stop Mum filling that house with Dutch migrants and hapless drifters.

She once told me a story of her horse, Silver, which pulled the milk cart her family used to deliver the milk and cream from their little dairy. Silver reared one morning and spilled all the milk cans. When my grandfather got home he was furious and he jumped on Silver and thrashed her all the way to Greensborough and back. The poor horse was in a lather of sweat and trembled from top to toe. Mum was inconsolable and even telling the story sixty-five years later poor Mum had tears rolling down her cheeks.

It wasn't Silver's fault, according to Mum, but my grandfather was a big knockabout bloke and had his theories on horse training. He spent a lot more time at agricultural shows than he did on the farm but when he was home he was boss. He churned through brownie points with his children but I idolised him. He showed me how to operate a carbide lamp and it was like the work of a magician. Those deep glowing lenses of ruby and emerald still appear in my dreams.

Poor Wangarabell had a terrible night. Vomiting, wandering around outside dazed. I walked with her as she tottered and fell. She had her head on one side just like her poor brother, Yambulla.

I watched over poor Bell but she really was removing herself from life. I had to leave her for a while so I could search the bush for orchid tubers and send some to archaeologist Judith Field for her research on the grinding stones at the Australian Museum. Some archaeologists have been a bit prickly since *Dark Emu* came out but Michael Westaway's Mithaka dig has changed the atmosphere quite a bit. When Judith asked for orchid bulbs I thought it was a great opportunity for the black and white sciences to work together. I look forward to her examination of the starch residues in the dishes. It will tell us so much about the diets of people from different regions.

When I first wanted to see the Cuddie Springs grindstone that I wrote about in *Dark Emu* there was quite a bit of resistance, but Liz Warning's charm enabled my access to the stones and I was able to look at them with the young Aboriginal researcher Laura McBride. The stone came from Laura's mother's Country so the museum's reluctance to allow her to see an artefact housed in the museum where she worked was deeply troubling.

Why were they so afraid? It was a really unfortunate impasse because when we were able to explain to the staff why we were interested in the stone they realised our interest was very close to theirs. The impediment was created because they felt they were the *owners* of the stone. I watched them as I explained that Laura's heritage meant that her great extended family owned the stone. I saw a light go on in a house where thousands had access to the switch for centuries.

Bell was really crook and I carried her onto my bed where she slept all night so soundly that I had to feel her heart from time to time. It was her best sleep for months and I realised how much warmth, comfort and reassurance she gained from the contact.

She was still wobbly and distressed in the morning and I knew the time had come but I had arranged to go up to Yambulla to meet with Jim Osborne and Cooma about Jim's offer to endow Gurandgi with a piece of land. It was such an important meeting for Yuin people that I could not let the moment pass.

I met Cooma near Walla Walla trail. We drove into the property and we were met by a large golden Mirrigan (dingo). This is dog dreaming Country, so Cooma and I looked at each other and stopped the car. The dingo walked toward the ute and sat down as if to formalise our access.

The dog kept looking over his shoulder and we knew there was another dog close by. Eventually we concluded the interview and began driving again. Soon there were two dingoes beside us and they followed us all the way into the property.

We visited a couple of the ceremonial sites we had seen before and speculated on where we might establish a Gurandgi camp. Jim arrived and we shook hands to fix our arrangement and discussed how we might care for the country together. Black and white in a compact of care.

Months later, when I returned to this site on my own to prepare the way for a Gurandgi lore camp, I was met by two Gungwan (emu) who walked in a complete circle around me as I worked. I went on with the job but the birds were so relaxed that they kept on eating blackberries as they sashayed about. On our way out of the camp a few months later I was escorted off the property by a Gungwan who ran in a slow and relaxed lope in front of me before turning on to the track where I had to turn right. The bird then disappeared as if by magic. These moments are precious to us. They are our contact with Country.

The beautiful Swordgrass Brown Butterfly

I thought about my own dog all the way back. I stopped when I got within phone reception and rang Wendy to help us with Bell. I met her at Lyn's place and the brave little dog got the green dream.

When Wendy had finished we took Bell back and buried her with her brother and planted a banksia above her. Both dogs now sprout banksias and soon will have the company of honeyeaters they knew when alive.

It is the season of butterflies. There are thousands of Common Brown but we have also seen the caterpillars of the Imperial Blue which swarm all over black wattle saplings.

This butterfly is incredibly beautiful and these little spirits give us comfort as the gap left by the dogs echoes so bleakly in the empty house.

The Family Christmas

The extended family have spread themselves over a few states and even to get the immediate family together is like droving cats. This year we decided to gather before Christmas and chose Warrnambool where my sister, Jen, lives as well as some mates of Lyn's.

We hired a big old house in the centre of town which had a timber balustrade that the kids kept polished quite well. On the way to Warrnambool I urged Lyn to tolerate my fascination with second-hand shops and I bought a few things including a mess of brass handles and knobs. I will get a lot of fun in finding places for them in the house.

We cooked and ate together, terrorised a restaurant or two, visited my sister and brother-in-law and then I hatched my plan of getting them all into the old Fletcher Jones garment factory.

We went to Gille and Jillian's 40th wedding anniversary, old dancing mates of Lyn's. The house was full of arthritic dancers and their kids who grew up together as a tribe. They're all in the photos of the eighties and nineties. The kids' parties were full of theatre, big on pirates and adventures and Cape Otway beaches.

I have to admit it was a kind of hell for me being surrounded by so many people all talking and laughing at once. Some people love it but I creep away into quiet corners and collect all the dogs who are usually in the same condition.

No dogs left now. It really is a raw nerve.

We got back to the farm just in time to help Joe, Evan and Shalah from the Maritime Union with a slab they are helping us build for our new grain shed. We need more room to store and process grain in hygienic conditions. The union have given us a jumpstart for the project.

The site we levelled for this shed must have been a factory site for the Yuin prior to the Invasion because this is where we found the edge ground axe which has become so precious to us. The farm turns up hundreds of artefacts after every probe into the soil. There is so much fish and other food on this place that it is obvious a large population called this place home.

I used some of the topsoil from the site to fill in holes in the road down near the stockyards and then slashed bracken. Gurandgi Simon came to the farm from Tasmania and we yarned about Uncle Max's anniversary and things we needed to do in preparation for the March lore camp. He's a good, earnest young man and it is so important that people like him follow and support the lore Uncle Max left for us.

It started raining and so the visiting Ganai fire mob from Orbost met in the lounge room and we talked about how we might influence VicForests to conduct low temperature burns to get the bush back to the state it was in before Europeans arrived. More like a garden than a forest, a food park.

We often worry about the risks of travel with Covid raging in the community and I got home from a shopping trip to Eden as crook as a dog. I did a RAT test but it was negative so I went out and did some slashing.

We had a BBQ for the fellas' Christmas break-up. We are so grateful for their dedicated work and we hope they have a great holiday with their families.

The weather is freezing cold and Bunjil is checking out the ducks which makes them nervous. The Nankeen Kestrel is plunging into the grass hunting small creatures very persistently until at last it experienced satisfaction. Dunnart?

While I was slashing down near the jetty I saw a large group of Yumburra on the swamp and a stately White Heron stalking amongst them. Up closer to the house this year's young Bunjil was harassing some Birran Durran Durran. The whole family on the farm seemed intent on food while I got off the tractor and couldn't bear the idea of cooking.

We were getting ready for lore camp and after twelve months of distress we can now look forward to ten days on Country in March. Rosco, Nathan and I did some rehearsal of some songs we've been working on to honour the Dingo Dreaming storyline which begins on the coast close to here and follows the rivers up to Yambulla and beyond. Terry and his father are important to that story and so we are determined to work through it carefully and respectfully.

Mirrigan (dingo) has often appeared when I have been at Yambulla. Their presence is strong there and we look forward to the time when the full story for that Country can be revealed.

All four of us visited the white ochre deposit near Eden to collect some clay for the camp. The site was pretty rugged so I stayed up on the headland and just stood looking out to sea. A dozen different birds came to enquire what I was up to and a very large hoverfly spent about ten minutes inspecting me. It was not at all intimidating but a chance for rest and reflection with Country.

Lyn's bushfire book, *Safer Forests Safer Homes*, came out that day and she spent her time distributing it to homes in the district. She was very anxious that people actually read it because the trauma from the 2019 fire is still palpable. The regrowth of wattles and tobacco bush has rendered the forest as dangerous as before the fire. We have to learn about caring for Country.

I get excited preparing for the visit of Marnie's mob around Christmas so I washed the boat, cleaned the oven, the car seats and slashed around the house. It is a warm day and I disturbed a huge black snake but managed to miss it with the tractor tyres.

I took the little blue paddle board out to the sandbar in the middle of the Wallagaraugh and had a lovely swim. I soak up the days when nobody is on the farm. December is very quiet on the river and so it was an hour of enormous calm, the calls of honeyeaters, monarchs, whistlers and flycatchers ringing out from the trees. And only me to hear them. It was so restful and I was full of gratitude.

On 24 December, Lyn and I travelled to Bega to pick up one of Lyn's rings which had broken. With Christmas presents in mind we drove on to Bermagui to visit a market but it consisted of beetroot and carrots so we cheered ourselves with a pide at the little cafe down the road. The bloke who runs that place cooks all the food and is perennially cheery so it's always a lovely thing to do. His potato and onion pide is a wonder.

When we got home the family had already arrived so we went for a swim and the shrill of children mingled with the bird calls. Whenever I hear those calls I am always reminded of Alia in the river hanging on to a paddle and singing as she stared up into the trees. The image has been indelibly stamped on my brain because it was the day I had to evacuate the family to Eden in 2019 as the fire descended on us.

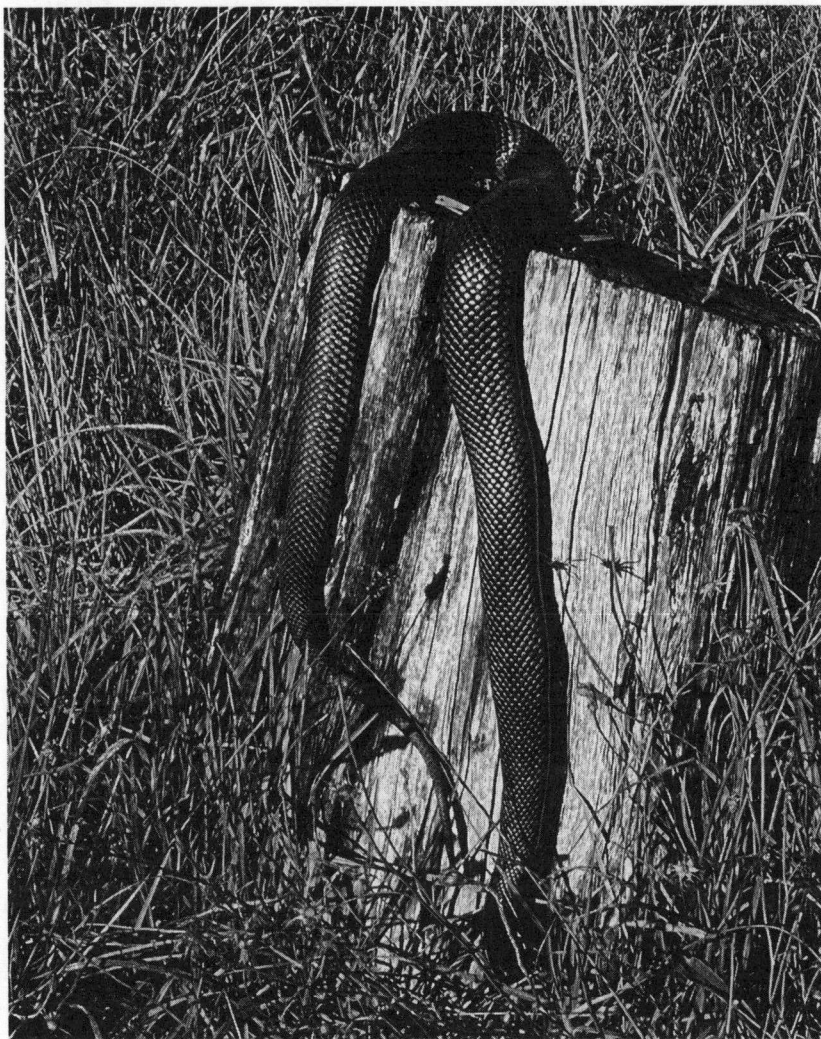

One of the resident black snakes soaking in the sun's warmth

I couldn't bear to think of those young voices being threatened by the roar of the fire I knew was coming. I had to work hard to convince the family to leave because they had already been evacuated that same day from Cape Conran.

The cabin they had booked burnt to the ground during the ferocity of that fire. It was in the same complex where we met to commemorate the massacre of Uncle Max's family on the Brodribb River. We had a naming ceremony there for Gurandgi children too. A lot of history lost with those buildings.

The silver tintinnabulation of Alia's singing was too much, the risk of harm too obvious, I had started to growl and pack people up. The Grumpy Grandad in full flight. The family was bemused and testy about my gruffness but we had to go.

The sky was a deep dark scarlet as we drove up the highway that day. We paid an exorbitant amount for a motel room along with half of Mallacoota's evacuated residents. The only things I brought from the farm were a painting Lyn gave me, the dogs and the possum skin rug the family made me.

I chucked the rug in the corner of the room which had only two beds. The dogs and I slept soundly on the rug. They never moved. Next morning the highway was full of cars leaving Eden as the sky was a tumulous of red and black smoke.

I hurried back to the room and started packing up the family once again and hustling them into the car and pushing them off to join the cavalcade. They were reluctant, but soon Marnie took charge and organised the evacuation of the whole motel to Canberra.

I asked Marnie to ring me every hour to tell me of their progress. True to her word she did and on one occasion Freddy was in my car and answered her call. 'Don't worry, Marnie, I'll look after him.' Such a great reassurance for Marnie, as Freddy had known Marnie from when she was a few weeks old. We both miss that man.

The memory of the rest of that day can still overwhelm me. I drove back to the farm with the road on fire and for the next six weeks we fought various fronts of the fire and battled to save houses. It is a nasty, distressing blur. I have to wrest my mind away from it so that we can enjoy the present.

Christmas day was a long, involved affair with Marlo as Father Christmas. We had breakfast and then, of course went for another swim. It was very hot and the water was glorious.

I hadn't finished cleaning the boat and all the little jobs I had planned because I was still lethargic with the flu.

Christmas on the river

Lyn and I went back to the house and started the preparations for the big Christmas lunch. We have cooked forty Christmas lunches together with a break of four years. I do the gravy, thank you Paul Kelly, because Lyn's system is so careful that you interrupt it at your peril. As always it was a wonderful meal.

Later I had to take Lyn back to Gipsy to let her chooks out and pick up another paddle for the kids. There was a lot more swimming and shrieking and I continued to tidy up the poor old neglected *Nadgee*. I am so busy I don't give her enough attention. She deserves more love as she is such an important partner in my life.

Boxing Day is always swimming and, for me, cricket. My devotion to the Test cricket is a mystery to the family but I really love the chess that cricket involves and, as an old bowler, I love to see the ball swing away from the right hander's bat. I dream of that moment. I could say more but I will desist.

Playing cricket was my day off and I miss it badly because now I struggle to find an excuse not to work. I called my father a work-horse in a story I wrote about him but the apple has fallen directly beneath that tree.

Anyway, there was more family swimming and we met up with Gab and Chris from Sailors Grave Brewing. We had the privilege of watching an osprey take a fish on the east bank of the Wallagaraugh. The osprey is rare here, so this was a memorable moment.

More swimming the next day. We all went down to Sandy Point on the Top Lake by boat. I got the old donut pumped up and Marlo and Alia had a great time being towed around. They are strong and fearless and keep urging me to do maximum speed. Poor old *Nadgee*.

It was a joy to see them so exhilarated. Charlee was next but the old donut gradually deflated and she was sunk. I felt really bad that the youngest couldn't have the same experience. I promised her I would buy a new donut. The old one had been patched more than

Yacob's pants, which is a song I had to sing in primary school on King Island. My teacher was Dutch and I loved her. I could still sing the song for you now if you like. Okay, I understand, let's move on.

I had to pump water up to the gravity feed tank so that we have fire protection and water for the gardens and house. It's a day long procedure so I stayed at home but the family went up to Davidson's Beach in Eden. They had a ball as usual but just as they were leaving Justin got stung by a stingray and they had to go up to Bega Hospital to check that the barb was not still in the wound.

They are regular customers at Bega Hospital as there are always falls and infections. Marnie is a nurse so nothing is left to chance. Justin was fine but very sore and the wound is quite large. When I was a teenager I was fishing for flounder with my brother-in-law when a stingray slashed my gumboot open. It didn't draw blood but I was always conscious thereafter of what they could do.

I heard that an old mate, Duncan Findlay, died yesterday. Mallacoota will not be the same. He was an irrepressible character, one of the funniest, most outrageous and irresponsible people I have ever met. He never failed to stop me in the street so that we could analyse the latest sport results, politics and old Mallacoota history.

Mallacoota is going to be a little drab without him but, as I said to some of the kids in town the other day, no one replaces Duncan, but you kids have to make your own history. There are enough ratbags around but they won't be the same ratbags and I'll never know any of them as long as I knew Duncan.

He claimed that Slim Dusty wrote the song 'Duncan' ('I love to have a beer with Duncan') after one of their escapades. Duncan seemed to have lived a dozen lives and was hugely entertaining about all of them but it doesn't mean I will ever forgive him for dropping two catches off my bowling at Wyndham in 1980!

I had a rest in the afternoon and listened to the swallows outside my window. They were roosting in the heat of the day and their conversation was entrancing. They spoke together in full sentences. One swallow was very talkative and the other responded in monosyllables. I'll let you do the gender profiling but I love those creatures, they are so much a part of my life. Their comfort is very important to me. Even last night one of the pair was roosting on the back door light which I turned on to warm it up while we had a heavy downpour.

Justin's foot improved enough for us to contemplate the adventure I had been planning for the kids for months.

NOTICE OF ADVENTURE

Able sea persons Marlo, Alia and Charlee are advised of the command to prepare for a voyage of exploration.

The purpose of the voyage is to discover the fresh waterfalls of the Wallagaraugh River in Far East Gippsland. The journey will necessitate sailing through the last farmland in the district, negotiating the shoals and the treacherous bar that are reputed to be in the vicinity. Once past the Bull Ring the aim is to traverse the river that disappears into jungle. Somewhere on the right there is said to be a lonely settlement. Once past that point, if indeed it exists, we will leave the jungles and navigate the giant boulders which lurk in the stream.

Finally, we will come, so they say, to a series of falls on a big bend. This last is just conjecture but, in the cause of science, it is our commission to investigate this phenomenon. It is reputed that snakes inhabit the region and a seal which tries to communicate with humans. If this beast exists we will have to describe its form and make sketches of its appearance.

For the purposes of the task, all sea persons must be equipped with broad hats and stout, waterproof shoes. Copious amounts of water in secure vessels will be required. Rations must be sufficient for the time allocated with enough remaining for the return voyage.

Sea persons are required to observe all birds and creatures of the deep but pay particular attention to the botany of this previously undescribed locale. Most particularly the existence of the fabled Wallagaraugh Grevillea will be of enormous interest to our scientific community and sea persons can expect generous rewards for its discovery.

Likewise, any evidence found of the Old People will be received with deep gratitude and rewards for this evidence are sure to flow.

Sleep well. No alcohol. Stout shoes. Clean underwear.

Captain Bitheega of the Lower Reaches
Yumburra Naval Precinct
By order of Bunjil

The journey up the river was incredible. The kids were tasked with finding certain things and they found the lot except the seal. The Wallagaraugh Grevillea flowers in spring so the chance of finding it in summer is unlikely but Marlo found both the plant and a flower on the plant.

We got to the freshwater falls and waded upstream to inspect them. *Nadgee* found a couple of the reefs of stone but we were travelling slowly so no harm was done. I found a piece of driftwood in a rock pool and thought of our friend Pat and her dogs. I wanted to make a memorial plaque for the dogs as Pat's second dog Omar died yesterday. We weren't to know that Pat would die a couple of days later.

(By the time I had the piece of timber at the farm I learnt of Pat's death and so she is included on the panel with her two dogs. I thank the kids for taking me to the place where I found that driftwood.)

We had a picnic on a sandy beach, a little downstream, and I heard Alia calling out, 'Pa, is this a scar tree?' I was having a little rest on the sand and got up, reluctantly, to have a look at the tree she was standing beside. At the back was an oval scar over a metre long. I think I first fished off that beach in 1973 and have visited it dozens of times since but have never seen that scar. I was struck dumb that it would be my granddaughter who found it in 2022. I am very proud.

I'd asked them to look for evidence of the First People thinking that they might find a flint or midden but Alia just went big time and found a coolamon scar. Later Charlee found a freshwater mussel shell which counted as a food item of the local people so I was really moved by their interest and care.

After we got back Marnie and Justin went to search for a piece of their car which fell off last night when they were coming back from the hospital. Their GPS directed them down Binns Road which is a potholed hell road. They did find the panel trim but also the wombat they must have clipped. Always upsetting.

I had hoped the seal would make an appearance while we were upstream but really, summer is not its season. The seal was young around 2002 when it learnt to recognise my boat motor. I might take off before dawn but the seal would find me and come to the side of the boat to say hello. When you're fishing you don't want the company of a fish-eating seal but it was such a character I could never resent its presence.

One time I was working on a small repair for *Nadgee* and the seal began diving beside me. It came up with a little silver elver, gave it a smart flick and tossed it into its mouth. It didn't exactly wink at me but it seemed pretty pleased with itself.

It dived like that for twenty minutes, always returning with a small eel and giving it the flick and toss treatment and then the sideways glance to see if I was suitably impressed.

We knew each other for a couple of decades. One night I was fishing up near Pine Corner on the Wallagaraugh and I caught my fish in twenty minutes, but it was such a beautiful night I dozed off with my head resting on the gunnel.

Suddenly there was a violent blast of air in my ear. That bloody seal had followed me all the way upstream. The water at the Corner is nearly fresh so it never occurred to me that she would come so far. Anyway, her presence meant the end of sleep and the disappearance of any fish in the vicinity.

While I was writing this book I saw her again. I assume it was the same animal because she made a great point of making sure I was watching her expertise. I was coming back from Gipsy and I saw a large body roiling close to the riverbank. The seal surfaced with a massive fish in her mouth. It might have been a ray because it was wide and its belly was snow white. The seal brought the catch up toward my boat and proceed to slap it with enormous violence on the surface of the water.

In between slaps the seal glanced up at me and assessed my admiration. It is hard for me not to think of it as the same seal. It might be a romantic thought or a wish for the longevity of a friend but, whatever the case, I enjoy the personality.

A male pelican used to visit me at the Gipsy jetty too. I would feed his family fish frames so we became close. The male bird took it into his head to wheel about and land on the jetty if ever he saw me there.

I rarely fish from the jetty so there was nothing for him to eat but he would waddle along the jetty and greet me, it seemed, with a loud graak graak graak and then settle himself beside me and swing his great beak around on to his back. Most of the time it wouldn't sleep but just regard me with that big yellow eye. The bird seemed not to defer to me, rather than confer with me. I hope I was up to scratch.

One autumn about six years ago I saw him leave with a large group when Lake Eyre was flooding and I haven't noticed him return. There are plenty of other pelicans about in summer but none who seek my company. I miss that silent communion.

The morning after the Wallagaraugh adventure I woke to the lovely splintery call of the Yellow-rumped Thornbill. I listened to the usual pardalotes and monarchs but there was also another bird calling which I couldn't recognise. I love knowing that there are still mysteries in the bush.

Charlee helped me tie up some tomatoes and do some weeding and install the white horse hose reel I bought at the Fletcher Jones market. I get so much pleasure out of resurrecting those old things and Charlee is a wonderful workmate.

I brought old friends Helen and David from Gipsy Point by boat to see what we were doing at the farm. I took them back in the *Nadgee* while the kids paddled down the river for Friday night drinks at the Gipsy Point jetty.

Gipsy Point goes through the normal generational cycles. Twenty years ago the town was dominated by middle-aged people of retiring age and now we have a new generation of grandchildren who dominate the town at this time of year.

The town installed a seat at the jetty for the comfort of tourists and we put a plaque in the middle of the back rail to commemorate an old resident. That was only a few years ago but the back of that four-seater park bench is now full.

We watch the kids bombing off the jetty as we eat our pies and drink our wine and beer. Those kids are so good with each other, so watchful of the young ones, but all so confident in the water. I love knowing my rather nervous grandchildren have this confidence and care surrounding them so they can risk doing things they might not do on their own.

Back at the farm the Buru have sorted out their order, so the days are serene now with the females and joeys lolling about. We enjoy the tender scenes as mothers groom the young. The young are sometimes caught between deciding whether to suckle or eat or try to coordinate their legs.

A young joey wonders about her next move

Lyn has been keeping an eye on a group where a big male is watching over the females and occasionally checking to see if a female will accept him. There is persistent tail scratching before he goes to the front of her and tries to touch her face. It is pretty obvious if she doesn't care to have her face touched. He checks anyway.

Next morning, where the big mob had been, there is just a male and female and a joey and Lyn is wondering if this is the same male as yesterday or a nuclear family separated from the alpha male and his harem.

Brave New Year

On the last day of the year we all went into town by boat and had breakfast at Amy's little cafe. Her dad, Presto, was doing the garbage run for her and so we had a yarn about the town. Presto is the mongrel who dropped me from the grand final this year. I haven't forgotten but I still talk to him.

Presto is as right-wing as Abbott but is a wonderful person. We don't vote the same but we talk the same. I miss that mad company. I went and watched one game during the season but I find it hard to watch my mates playing. It was the same with footy, I watched about two games but I was jealous. It's a terrible emotion but I just couldn't enjoy watching my mates having fun.

The family walked through the summer market. I paid all the kids for their Voyage of Discovery and they walked about making assessments of value. Alia is into saving so her wages went straight into her deepest pocket. Charlee bought a bracelet and a hippy cushion, she is a girl with firm opinions about style.

I helped Lyn make pizzas in the pizza oven she made fifteen years ago. We took the pizzas down to the jetty for another celebration with the Gipsies. More splashing and swimming and I know I'll grieve for the mayhem as soon as it stops.

I left at about 8.30 and sailed back to the farm thinking of all the people who have passed in recent years. I don't think it was gloom, more like reflection on the passing of time and souls. I listened to the weird call of the White-throated Nightjar, a bird with whom I am very close.

I saw one roosting on the ground in a spread of Round Leaf Box leaves on the top of the ridge at Maramingo in the seventies and I was riveted at seeing such a wild and cryptic creature.

I backed away but couldn't take my eyes from the shape hidden in the Persian carpet of golden leaves. When the Round Leaf Box drops leaves they go a lovely range of European autumn shades. A grove of these trees is one of the most serene places on Earth. I still dream of that ridge.

I continued to listen to the Nightjar and concentrated on the warm air, waiting for a shift of air, a zephyr, Kurru Kurrai wind spirit. At last there was the feathery movement of breeze I had been waiting for and I used it to talk to Uncle Max about the difficulty of keeping the Gurandgi together. He said nothing but I felt that wry smile.

I was grateful for that warmth because these last years have worn me down. I don't experience happiness in the same way as I did before. I am much more guarded and I don't like that caution, it never used to be part of me.

But I think there is a big change coming. I meet so many people who want to embrace the full history of the country. Aboriginal history is Australian history, the future of Aboriginal people is the future of all Australians.

I believe a large majority want Aboriginal people to be included in the Constitution but will they also insist that Aboriginal people are included in the wealth made from the capital Aboriginal people invested in the land?

On the farm we have seen firsthand how some people proclaim their support and love for Aboriginal people and insist on their love and understanding of our culture, oh you wise and beautiful people … only to find that sentiment is wafer thin. It's all about them. They want to salve their conscience while protecting their wallet.

I think my skin is paper thin these days, the slightest abrasion and I bleed. My toughness and endurance fading.

I didn't speak to Uncle Max again that night but I was with him and I was grateful for the communion.

Night closes in on the farm

The following day the kids were learning to do handstands, cartwheels and backward flips on the paddle board. It thrilled me, of course, but the thrill was muffled, a siren call to a deaf man, deadened, snatched away by the wind and time.

I try not to think like this but perhaps it's time I did. I love the world deeply but we cannot demand her eternal comfort.

Language Glossary

Barunguba
also known as Montague Island, is just off the coast of Narooma, NSW. It is a culturally significant Yuin place.

Biamanga
also known as Mumbulla Mountain; a sacred Yuin site in NSW, Biamanga is a landmark that can be seen through-out the Bega Valley.

Bidwell-Maap
Country and Traditional Owners of the area between Ganai and Yuin in Far East Gippsland.

Bimbla
Blood Mussel

Binyaroo
Little Black Cormorant

Birran Durran Durran
Plover or Masked Lapwing

Bodalla
Wallaby

buna
knoll (dance ground)

Bunjil
Wedge-tailed Eagle

Bura
fish

Buru
kangaroo

Buru Ngalluk
Kangaroo Grass; a tufted native Australian grass that can be used to make flour.

cobberer
Teredo worms; a mollusc found in saltwater, they were a favourite food of Aboriginal people in the Gipsy Point area.

Coolabah
Eucalyptus tree, native to Australia.

coolamon
Wiradjuri word for a wooden dish or vessel commonly used for water or food.

coolamon scar
a unique mark or scar seen on trees that have had bark stripped away to make a coolamon.

cumbungi
Wiradjuri word for Bulrush; native Australian aquatic plant found in swamps, billabongs, lakes, wetlands, drains, dams and lagoons.

cunjim winyu
a herb that grows at the edges of the salt swamp; the Yuin word translates to 'salty sun'.

Dalgal
Black Mussel

Dangar
damper or bread

Dharug
Country and the Traditional Owners of the area from the Blue Mountains to the sea in the east and from the Hawkesbury River to Appin in the south.

Dulumunmun
short legs; one of Uncle Max's names.

Gadu
ocean

Galoo
White-faced Heron; tall water bird sometimes called Blue Crane.

Ganai
Traditional Owners of the area from Warragul to the Snowy River in the east and from the Great Divide in the north to the coast in the south.

Garragagan
west wind

Garramagang
magpie

Garrara Ngalluk
Spear Grass; a sparsely tufted native Australian grass that can be used to make flour.

Giyong Budjarn
Welcome Swallow

Googar
goanna

Googoonyella
kookaburra

Goomera
Brush-tailed Possum

Grandfather Sun
name that shows respect for the Sun that provides light and warmth and fosters life.

Grandmother Moon
name that shows respect for the Moon that moves the ocean and affects the tides.

Gunditjmara
the Traditional Owners of the area from Portland in the south, Port Fairy, Warrnambool and inland into Camperdown.

Gungwan
emu

Gunyu
swan

Gurandgi
Aboriginal lore group within Yuin Country that was formed by Uncle Max Harrison.

Gurawul
whale

Jitti Jitti
Willy Wagtail

Jungaa
octopus

Kina
sea urchins

Koon ar rook
Wood Duck

Kuboka
Grey Shrikethrush

Kurru Kurrai
wind spirit

Kuuku Ya'u
Traditional Owners of Cape York who have had native title rights recognised for over 10 square kilometres of land in the area.

Mamadyan Ngalluk
Dancing Grass; a native Australian millet that can be used to make flour.

Maramingo
fish spear; also the name of a creek.

Maran
seagull

Mirragunegin
place of the dogs; the name of a mountain in Yambulla.

Mirridar
Sea Eagle

Mirrigan
dog

Mirrigan
dingo

Munyang
Vanilla Lily; native Australian edible root of a vanilla-scented flower. Slightly sweet, can be eaten raw or roasted and commonly found on the east coast of Australia.

Murnong
Yam Daisy; native Australian edible root of a yellow flower plant that's similar to parsnip. It was a commodity among Aboriginal people in southern parts of Australia.

Nenak
Yellow-tailed Black Cockatoo

Nullamaa
north

Nyaampa
Country is south of the Barwon and Darling rivers, from Brewarrina to Dunlop, including Yanda Creek down to Mulga Creek and the Bogan River.

Rainbow Serpent
Creator Spirit known for creating waterways. The Rainbow Serpent is known by different names in different Countries and while the story has some variations, the essence of this Creator Spirit remains the same: life-giving through rain but when not respected can cause drought or floods.

Walkun
abalone

Wathaurong
Country and the Traditional Owners of the area from the Great Dividing Range to the coast in the south and from the Werribee River to Aireys Inlet, with around 25 clans that are a part of the Kulin nation.

Wiradjuri
Country and the Traditional Owners of the area from the Great Dividing Range in the east, Hay and Nyngan in the west, Gunnedah in the north and Albury to the south.

Wurundjeri
Traditional Owners of the area known today as Melbourne in Victoria.

Yedding
Moon

Yorta Yorta
Country and Traditional Owners of the area on both sides of the Murray River from Cohuna to Albury/ Wodonga and north to just south of Deniliquin and south to just north of Euroa.

Yuin
Country covers the area from Shoalhaven in the north to Eden in the south.

Yumburra
Black Duck

Acknowledgements

We would like to thank Chris, Mark, Terry, Nathan, Mook, Cal, Sean, Uncle Noel and Trish, Lindsay, Chris S, Kate and all who have worked on the farm. We would also like to acknowledge family and friends who appear in the book.

And, of course, the Country herself.

Bruce Pascoe and Lyn Harwood have lived and worked in the area of the Three Salt Rivers for decades and are grateful to Country and the chance to honour her in words, photos, drawings and ceremony.